BUILDING TOMORROW'S TALENT

A PRACTITIONER'S GUIDE TO TALENT MANAGEMENT AND SUCCESSION PLANNING

MATTHEW GAY, SPHR

DORIS SIMS, SPHR

Bloomington, IN   authorHOUSE   Milton Keynes, UK

AuthorHouse™
1663 Liberty Drive, Suite 200
Bloomington, IN 47403
www.authorhouse.com
Phone: 1-800-839-8640

AuthorHouse™ UK Ltd.
500 Avebury Boulevard
Central Milton Keynes, MK9 2BE
www.authorhouse.co.uk
Phone: 08001974150

First published by AuthorHouse 01/25/07

ISBN: 978-1-4259-9465-5 (sc)

Printed in the United States of America
Bloomington, Indiana

To Katie, Taylor and Lauren
Thank you for giving me at least 207 reasons to smile every day.
You make this a wonderful world!

To my mother,
Thank you for being my biggest cheerleader!

To Joe and Jeff,
Thank you for always pushing me beyond my limits.
- M. G.

To Marilyn and Eldon, and to Jeremy and Spencer,
who surround me full circle with love.

To Diana and Julie,
Thank you for your friendship and for
always being there for me – you are the best!
- D. S.

Table of Contents

Book Purpose

The purpose of this book is to provide practical advice, ideas, and planning tools to create and implement processes for the assessment of the leadership team within your organization.

This book does not provide legal advice. Readers are advised to work with professional legal counsel to review and approve all talent assessment, succession planning, and leadership development strategic plans, processes and programs created, modified, and/or implemented within their own organizations.

About the Authors

Doris and Matthew have 35 years of combined experience in the areas of human resources, organizational development, recruiting, leadership development, call center training, and systems training, and 10 combined years of experience specifically in the area of talent management.

Doris and Matthew have worked as internal human resource practitioners in multiple Fortune 500 companies and in global organizations, with industry experience in finance, hospitality, healthcare, telecommunications, information services, and manufacturing.

Matthew received his Masters degree in the field of Human Resource Development from the University of Oklahoma (Go Sooners!), and Doris received her Masters degree in Human Resource Development from Indiana State University (Go Sycamores!). Their Talent Management processes and ideas have been documented as best practices by the Corporate Leadership Council.

Both authors have achieved their SPHR – Senior Professional in Human Resources – certification. They both enjoy speaking at national and international conferences and talking with anyone who is interested in the topic of Talent Management!

We welcome you to our web site, www.BuildingTomorrowsTalent.com, to contact us and to view more talent management resources.

Acknowledgements

We are incredibly grateful to the many people who have provided encouragement, ideas, hours of proofreading time, and patience during the creation of this book. While many people have contributed to this book over our lifetimes and our careers, there are several people we would like to acknowledge who have contributed in a special way to this book.

Special and heartfelt thanks go to Joe Ellison, SPHR – our friend, mentor, editor, advisor, and human resources genius. Thank you for your countless hours providing an enormous amount of feedback and ideas that have greatly enhanced this book. Your selfless approach in giving your time and energy to help others is amazing and inspiring to others.

We gratefully acknowledge the advice, ideas, encouragement, and proofreading time provided by Susan Steinbrecher, Cassandra Criswell, PHR and Mark Caruso.

A special thank you goes to artist Chris Morris, who created an imaginative book cover and illustrations for our section pages that add a fun aspect to our book!

We thank our family members and friends who demonstrated ongoing patience listening to us talk about this book many times, and provided the support and energy we needed to make this book a reality.

Preface

(Otherwise known as the chapter no one reads...but you should read this one.)

Every day organizations throughout the world make decisions to invest dollars and resources for the purpose of increasing revenue or reducing expenses. These decisions are never easy – especially when they involve someone's employment, advancement, or development. Talent management pertains to making an investment in people development, by identifying successors and talented individuals to develop for leadership roles in the organization.

More companies today are making the decision to formally and regularly review their talent and to identify successors for current and future positions. Traditionally, companies have allocated time and funding in other formal planning endeavors – negotiating annual budgets, creating marketing plans, and forecasting sales projections. Today, companies are taking the time to forecast their current and future talent needs, recognizing that their people are truly a critical differentiator between competing organizations, and not just a nice thing to say to employees to increase morale. In addition, globalization and changing workforce demographics increase the business need for effective talent management processes.

Talent management pertains to the identification, development, and career movement of employees and leaders within the organization, to increase retention of key talent and to prepare leaders with a wide breadth of knowledge and cross-functional skills. Every manager can think of critical employees who left the company without a successor, and the resulting gaping knowledge and skill holes that were left in their absence. The most effective managers take the time to identify successors, provide development and cross-training opportunities, and work towards internal retention and career movement to minimize talent vacancy impact.

In the past, employees used to continue their career with one company for many years, often moving in a steady, progressive manner "up the ladder" as their company tenure increased. Today, career development is more complicated. A corporation's talent strategies need to revolve around continuous skill and knowledge development, leadership preparation, and retention of the organization's most talented employees. Progressive corporations today understand the importance of continuously preparing and developing their people for the future growth of the organization.

As companies are identifying this need for talent and succession management, they are often tapping individuals in the organization to lead this effort for the first time. If you are beginning a talent and succession management initiative for the first time, this book is designed to provide a step-by-step creation process that enables you to choose the components and plans that best fit your organization's culture, size, and situation. If you have an established program in place, this book provides an opportunity to consider new and additional components to your talent management strategy.

This book has been created to assist you as you construct and execute your plans for talent and succession planning, whether you are implementing one aspect of talent management, such as high potential identification and development, or implementing an entire new talent management strategy.

As you create or update your talent management program, remember that your work today will have an impact in the career development of future leaders and key players in your company for many years to come. Shareholders expect short-term results for positive financial returns, and long term results to carry on a legacy for decades. This type of long-term success requires a prepared leadership pipeline and the retention of highly skilled individuals, especially in service and technology industries where the key differentiation between competitors is the human talent and intellectual capital.

As you work on your talent management initiatives, there may be times when you become discouraged as you hit potential road blocks such as, "Will we tell a high potential employee that they have been identified as high potential?" or, "Won't this create an elitist group in our company?" or the classic line, "We don't have time for this." Create contingency plans and responses for these questions (because you will hear them), and continue to work towards your long-term goal of formal, consistent, and organizational-wide talent reviews and succession plans.

Just remember, as everyone else is running around in the company making a buck today, you are working to retain and prepare the key talent who will be running around the company making the bucks 5 years, 10 years, and 20 years or more from now!

Matthew Gay and Doris Sims

How To Use This Book

(Or, how to really get your money's worth out of this book...)

What This Book Is Not About

This book is not another theory or research book. It is not a massive book that is best used for pressing leaves for that science project or for toddlers to sit on at the Thanksgiving meal. It is not a book that only pertains to large organizations with large budgets. It is not a book of dry reading material that will cure your insomnia.

What This Book Is About

This book was created for anyone who has been asked to create or update a succession planning and talent management process within their organization. It has been created for those of you who have just been asked to put together a high potential identification and development strategy and are wondering where to start. It has been created for those of you who are reviewing talent management on-line systems and you are updating your internal processes before customizing your system. And it has been created for those of you who want to work with your business leaders to have regular and structured meetings to discuss the career development of your future leaders. This book has been designed to be a workbook that will take you from your first planning steps to the point of measuring and communicating results and action plans.

The Ultimate Goal

To provide user-friendly tools to create a simple talent management and succession planning process that will have the most significant business impact.

Go With the Flow...

If you need this book to help you with one aspect of talent management, of course you will want to just go directly to that chapter. But if you are using this book to put together a new talent management strategy for your company, this diagram provides an overview of the potential steps you can follow as you are creating your Talent Management design:

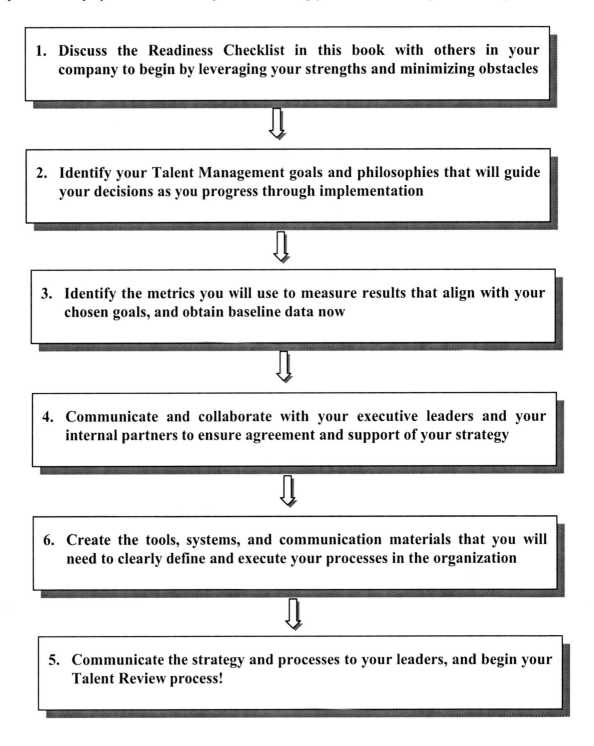

1. **Discuss the Readiness Checklist in this book with others in your company to begin by leveraging your strengths and minimizing obstacles**

2. **Identify your Talent Management goals and philosophies that will guide your decisions as you progress through implementation**

3. **Identify the metrics you will use to measure results that align with your chosen goals, and obtain baseline data now**

4. **Communicate and collaborate with your executive leaders and your internal partners to ensure agreement and support of your strategy**

6. **Create the tools, systems, and communication materials that you will need to clearly define and execute your processes in the organization**

5. **Communicate the strategy and processes to your leaders, and begin your Talent Review process!**

Building Tomorrow's Talent Toolkit

The following tools are provided in this book, to help you create a complete project implementation plan for your Talent Management initiative:

❑ **Readiness Checklist:** This tool is provided to help you work with others in your company to identify the drivers and the potential obstacles that will be influential factors as you implement your Talent Management strategy. You can use this checklist during your initial planning meetings to facilitate initial strategy discussions.

❑ **Checkpoints:** At the end of each chapter in the Planning Section of this book, a "Checkpoint" has been provided to help you summarize your goals and decisions.

❑ **Sample Executive Presentation Slides:** To help you get started when you are ready to create a Talent Management strategy presentation for your senior leaders, sample slides are included in this book.

❑ **Metrics Checklist:** This tool provides a wealth of ideas for potential metrics that can be used to measure the results of your Talent Management initiative. The metrics are divided into categories to help you select the applicable metrics from each area of measurement.

❑ **Project Summary Tool:** At this end of this book, you will find a form that is designed to summarize all of the goals, actions, and decisions you will be making as you work your way through each chapter. A completed Project Summary Tool will provide the basis for a formal project plan or proposal to use in your organization either for approval or communication purposes.

If You Need More Help...

We hope you find this book to be easy to use, to the point, and thorough. We will also be adding a bit of humor from time to time, to keep things interesting and fun. If you have questions along the way, you can contact us through our web site at: www.BuildingTomorrowsTalent.com. We'll be impressed that you read every page of *How to Use This Book*, and we'll be happy to answer a question.

Terms and Definitions

(Or, what do we mean when we say...)

360-Feedback – A survey and/or interview process designed to obtain feedback from those who work and interact with an individual on a regular basis. Typically, feedback is obtained from the individual's leader, peers, direct reports, and internal or external customers. Some organizations use the 360-feedback process strictly as a development tool; others use this process for performance appraisals or as an assessment tool.

Blocker – This term is sometimes used to describe a leader who is thought to be at the peak of their leadership career, with high potential employees reporting to him or her. The "blocker" is typically a solid performer with low future potential. High potential employees in the group may perceive a lack of advancement opportunity within their business group due to the "blocker".

High Performer – An employee who consistently demonstrates superior work performance, but does not currently demonstrate a strong ability or desire for rapid advancement, career challenges and risks, and/or leadership roles.

High Potential – A High Performer employee who also consistently demonstrates superior work performance and also displays a strong potential, ability, and desire for rapid advancement into leadership roles, as well as being open to new career challenges and learning opportunities.

Typically, high potentials are considered to be only the top 1-5% of the organization in terms of achieving business results, demonstrating high learning agility and innovation, handling change and stress effectively, and exhibiting excellent interpersonal skills.

Leader – In this book, we will use this term to refer to anyone in a formal management position, ranging from a supervisor to the CEO.

Leadership Benchstrength – Refers to the competency and readiness levels of leaders to grow with the organization and to be prepared for new leadership roles. Organizations with a strong leadership benchstrength have multiple successors actively developing in the pipeline (both short and long term successors) to fill current and future leadership roles.

Leadership Competencies – The knowledge, skills, and abilities attributed to effective leaders, defined by the organization to reflect the leadership values, culture, and business needs of the company. Typically, an organization identifies a specific set of leadership competencies that are unique to the organization's culture, business needs, and values.

Learning Agility – Learning agility encompasses the ability to learn very quickly and think creatively. Individuals with high learning agility also seek out the ideas and feedback of others, and work towards continuous improvement both for personal effectiveness and team effectiveness. Demonstrating high learning agility includes the ability to be flexible,

handle stress well, and adapt to change. Individuals with hig
effectively in ambiguous situations.

Nine-Box Performance/Potential Management – A nine-box chart provides a cross-reference view of both the current performance level and the future potential estimate of individuals within the organization.

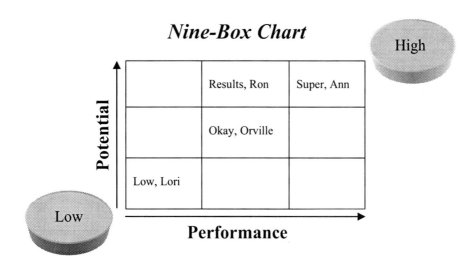

Performance Management – This term refers to all organizational processes associated with communicating performance objectives and measuring performance results. This includes establishing work goals, providing feedback and coaching, and the company's performance review process.

Performance Review – The practice of evaluating and discussing an individual's past performance, behaviors, and the achievement of work goals, typically using a rating scale and written comments. Most organizations conduct formal performance review processes on an annual, semi-annual, or quarterly basis.

Replacement Planning – This term is used to define the process of identifying potential replacement candidates for current incumbent leaders. It is considered to be a basic level of succession planning and succession management – one that does not include identifying future leadership positions, future leadership pools, successor competency gaps and development needs, etc.

Talent Assessment – The process of reviewing and appraising employees regarding their future potential in the organization, based on factors such as past performance, leadership ability, learning agility, advancement potential, advancement desire, competencies, and skill sets.

Talent Management – Facilitating the development and career progress of highly talented and skilled individuals in the organization, using formalized procedures, resources, policies, and processes. The Talent Management process focuses on developing employees and leaders for the future of the organization.

Talent Review Meeting – In this book, the Talent Review meeting refers to a facilitated meeting attended by business unit leaders and human resource leaders (in small organizations or when reviewing top executive talent, this meeting may take place with one business unit leader).

During the Talent Review meeting, the strengths and development needs of leaders within the business unit are discussed. Other potential topics of the Talent Review meeting include next potential career moves, position vacancy risks, future leadership position needs, and leadership abilities for each leader. Talent Review meetings may also include succession plan discussions, and reviewing high potential nominations and talent management information.

Succession Management – Succession management includes succession planning (defined below), as well as all continuous actions and processes throughout the year regarding the development of successors. Succession management also involves looking ahead at the leadership competencies and positions that will be needed for the organization's future success, rather than only looking at replacement needs.

Succession Planning – Planning the potential replacements of current leader positions. This may include identifying those who are fully qualified for the incumbent's position, those who are expected to be ready within a specified number of years, and/or those who are expected to be ready once specific competencies are developed (without indicating a time period of readiness).

Section One: The Planning Stage
Developing Your Strategy

Building Your Leadership Pipeline

In the practice of Talent Management, practitioners often talk about building their leadership pipeline, but what does that really mean?

Think of a successful sales group. They will have new customer markets they are just looking into, potential customers they are contacting for the first time, prospective customers who they are actively selling to, customers they are about to close the deal with, and current customers.

The Sales Pipeline

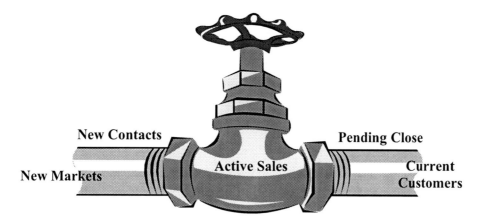

New Contacts

Pending Close

New Markets

Active Sales

Current Customers

Consider what would occur if there were any gaps in the sales pipeline. If new markets are not pursued, eventually the current markets will become saturated. New customer contacts are needed to identify customers to pursue for active sales actions for the organization to continue to grow. If there are no pending sales, the entire company (and the shareholder population) becomes nervous about the organization's future financial condition.

The same concept applies to building your leadership pipeline. It is important to review and develop current individual contributors who could be your next front-line supervisors and managers. You will want to develop current leaders to broaden their scope, strategic thinking, and people skills, for preparation for higher-level, more complex positions. Developing your senior leader team will help prepare your future top executives.

The process of developing leaders within each stage of this pipeline takes years. For example, depending on the current readiness level of your current leadership team, it may take 5-10 years and multiple cross-functional job assignments to develop your next executive level leaders.

An organization that is prepared for the future will work at ensuring there are no gaps in their leadership pipeline. As with the sales pipeline, if the talent management and development programs do not address each leadership group, eventually a performance and financial weakness may occur in the organization. A performance issue may occur when leaders moving to the next level of leadership are not adequately prepared. A financial weakness may occur due to missed business opportunities, and due to the high costs of recruiting external leadership and executive talent.

The Leadership Development Pipeline

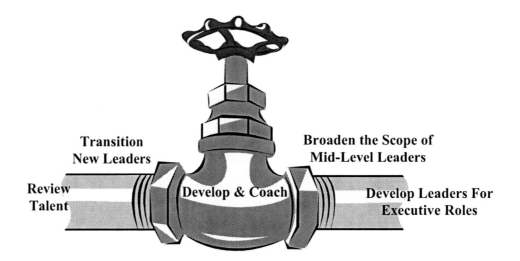

A strong leadership pipeline includes the identification, retention, and development of leadership talent at each leadership level, including those who are not yet in leadership roles.

Leadership Benchstrength

When an organization has multiple prepared individuals at each of these pipeline stages, and is able to retain these individuals and keep their level of engagement in the company at a high level, the organization is said to have a solid "leadership benchstrength".

The actions a company takes to build its leadership benchstrength vary greatly depending on the size, structure, and type of organization. The key idea is to take action, remembering that once the organization experiences a gap in the pipeline, performance and financials suffer.

Because organizations have many needs that require financial funding, most companies do not have an unlimited supply of leadership development resources to spend equally on every employee at every level in the company. For this reason, the Talent Review and Succession Planning process described throughout this book assists the organization in focusing on employees who have the most potential for leadership roles in the organization.

Sometimes an organization realizes they have one or more current or future gaps in their leadership pipeline, but does not know how to address it. There are actually many actions a company can take within the organization to build their leadership benchstrength, including on-the-job development, formal development programs, job rotational assignments, mentor programs, etc. Organizations also use an external talent acquisition talent strategy to fill leadership gaps and to bring in new talent and business opportunities.

Leadership Development Actions

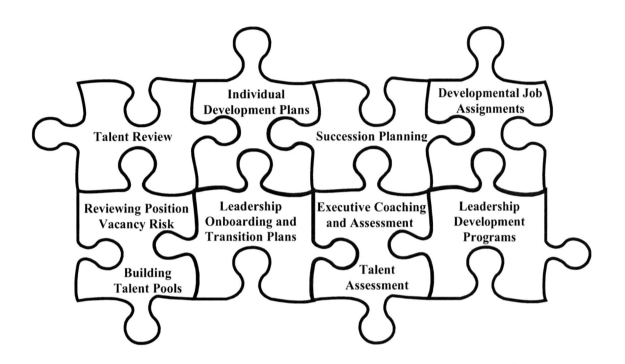

An Overview of a Talent Management Sample Process

In this book, we will focus primarily on the following four leadership development actions:

- **Talent Assessment** – the process of rating individuals in the organization in a formal, quantifiable manner, assessing them on both past performance and future potential.

- **Talent Review** – the process of reviewing individuals in the organization in a structure, qualitative manner, using a formal group discussion methodology.

- **Succession Planning** – the process of identifying individuals who are prepared to fill current incumbent leadership positions now, as well as identifying individuals who have the potential to fill these positions in the future, and identifying action plans to address competency or qualification gaps.

- **Identification of High Potentials** – the process of identifying individuals who demonstrate the ability and desire to advance rapidly in leadership roles in the organization. These individuals will receive increased visibility, development, and career opportunities, in an effort to accelerate their readiness to move into new leadership roles.

NOTE: Although the development of successors and high potentials is a critical part of the Talent Management and Leadership Development functions of the organization, the focus of this book will be on the strategic planning and identification process that pertains to the four leadership development actions listed above. These four actions alone provide more than enough content for you to consider, to discuss with colleagues, and to implement, for one book!

It is difficult to provide a "generic" Talent Management process, because each organization will make different choices regarding the components and procedures that meet their strategic goals. And, at this point, the Talent Management specialty area is still emerging, and many aspects of this area are still lacking clear "best practices" or "standard procedures".

Therefore, the diagram on the following page provides an overview of the Talent Management process that is represented throughout the remainder of this book.

Sample Talent Management Annual Process

The first section of this book pertains to the strategic planning that must take place prior to implementing a Talent Management process for the first time in an organization. The diagram below represents a sample annual Talent Management process that will take place in an organization throughout the year. The diagram assumes all strategic planning and the creation of tools required for the process have already been completed.

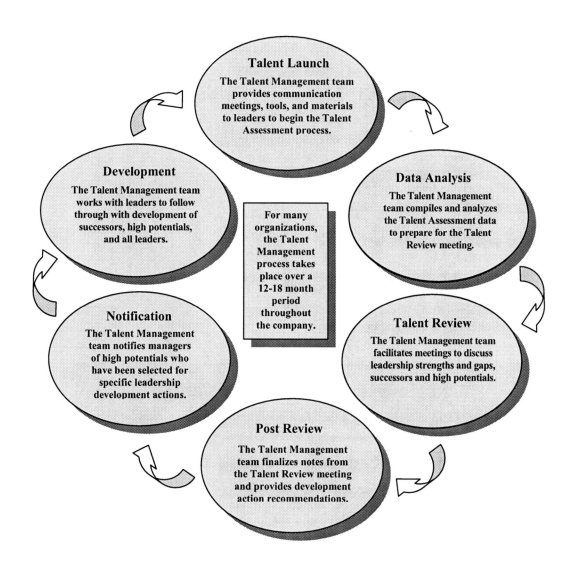

Planning for Results

The time you will be taking to create your strategic plan for Succession Planning and/or Talent Management processes is the most critical period of the project. Philosophies and best practices surrounding these types of programs vary widely, and it will be important for you to ensure that the policies and processes you create match your business needs. You will want to create a talent management and succession planning program that fits the needs of your own company, factoring in your:

- ❑ Emerging business strategies – new products, markets, and services

- ❑ Organization's size

- ❑ Geographic locations (is your organization local, national, or global?)

- ❑ Culture

- ❑ Leadership competencies (current and future leadership needs and values)

- ❑ Current leadership demographics

- ❑ Leadership development budget

- ❑ Organizational growth rate

- ❑ Available staff to plan and implement the program

This section includes information and checklists to help you sort through a multitude of ideas and options that are available to you.

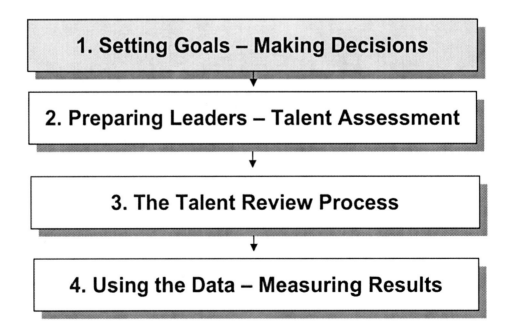

1. Setting Goals – Making Decisions

↓

2. Preparing Leaders – Talent Assessment

↓

3. The Talent Review Process

↓

4. Using the Data – Measuring Results

As you continue reading and working through the book, you will make changes to your original plan, and you will be working to create your timeline and project plan. At the end of the book, use the Project Planning tool to help you finalize your strategy.

What Questions Will Be Answered?

In the Planning section of this book, you will find answers to the following questions:

❏   How can I tell if my organization is ready for these programs?

❏   What are the most critical readiness factors I should see in my organization before I begin to implement these programs?

❏   What personnel resources (at minimum) will I need?

❏   What goals should I set for our program for both the short term and the long-term success of our strategy?

❏   Does our organization want to just implement Succession Planning processes, Talent Management and High Potential Identification processes, or both?

❏   What advantages and disadvantages of implementing a high potential program do other companies perceive?

❏   What decisions should all key stakeholder of this project agree upon up front, before proceeding with implementation?

Whether you are implementing a new program, or updating a current one, the information in this section will help reduce the time and risk involved in a "trial and error" approach, by helping you think through your choices, and talking with other project stakeholders, before moving forward with your plans.

Chapter One

Are You Ready?

If you are reading this chapter, it may be because someone in your company has approached you already to either implement a new Talent Review and Succession Planning process, or to update your current process, so that in itself is the first indicator of readiness – your organization recognizes the need for this program. Perhaps a critical leader just left the company with a gaping hole that the company is not prepared to fill. Perhaps the CEO read an article or talked with a colleague about the importance of succession planning.

Or, maybe the organization is looking at the number of senior leaders who will be eligible to retire in the next few years. Or, you may have seen the need for Talent Management in your organization and you are beginning to implement this strategy yourself. So we know at least one person in your organization is interested in launching this program!

This chapter identifies the first actions you need to take before your Talent Review and Succession Planning programs are launched. You will need to:

- o Identify Sponsors

- o Gather Information

- o Define Your Goals

- o Define Your Talent Review Philosophies

- o Prepare Your Organization

- o Identify Resources

- o Establish Leadership Accountability for Leadership Development

- o Complete the Readiness Checklist

Identify Executive-Level Sponsors

So then the next question is, who will sponsor this effort, providing funds, resources, personnel, and motivators for leaders to follow through with their actions? Most people will tell you that if you don't have the sponsorship of the CEO, then don't even bother trying to start this initiative. While you certainly need and benefit from the sponsorship of the CEO, you may not have this initially, and that is not a reason to give up. However, it is important that your CEO is aware of the process, and provides the approval and funding of the program to move forward.

You may not have the sponsorship of the CEO initially because he or she doesn't really know much about this type of process – this is not unusual at all. It just means you are going to have to demonstrate a solid level of value from it within the first year, which you can do. Listed below are some examples of value you can conceivably demonstrate within the first year. Take a minute to check the items you think would be applicable to your company and are potentially achievable for you:

- ◻ Decrease the cost of external hires for leadership positions in the company by increasing internal hires (through lateral and promotional career moves)

- ◻ Retention of high potentials and successors

- ◻ Having the right talent in place to achieve specific business goals

- ◻ The value the business unit leaders perceive that they derive from the process. For example, they may value learning more about talent in their departments, identifying and developing successors, identifying potential weak areas or poor performers in the leadership team, etc.

- ◻ Shorter "time-to-fill" for leadership positions

- ◻ A shorter "learning curve" time period for new leaders who have been developed and prepared for management positions

- ◻ Proactively communicating to customers, analysts, and other stakeholders that the organization has a formal succession planning process (some customers may even ask for information about your company's succession planning process

You may not have the sponsorship of the CEO because there are already too many other priorities and initiatives going on in the company for him or her to even focus on this. If this is the case, then it may not be a good idea to launch the program this year; it depends on the number of and critical nature of the other priorities. However, even if you don't launch talent management processes in the first year, you can use the time to benchmark, discuss options, and plan your strategy and tools.

You may not have the initial sponsorship you need because the leadership team is not yet familiar with talent management, high potential development, succession management, etc. Remember, these human resource actions are still emerging and taking shape within the corporate environment.

You may not receive full "buy-in" until <u>after</u> the launch of your program, after your leaders have an opportunity to see and experience a Talent Assessment process and a Talent Review meeting. To date, we have ALWAYS received positive feedback from leaders after they experience these processes for the first time that these talent management actions are very valuable and important to the business, *even when the meeting began with doubt and even suspicion about the process.*

It is important to remember that it takes several years to develop mid-level leaders into strong senior-level leaders, and for senior-level leaders to develop into highly effective successors. Therefore, if you have a large population of senior leaders retiring over the next 5-10 years, it is important to go ahead and present your business case for implementing the program as a top priority for the company.

Sometimes, the success of implementing talent management processes is affected by other important and urgent business needs and goals. Take a minute to list the business priorities going on in your company right now, and then evaluate these to determine, if you were the CEO or a member of your executive team, how you would view the priority level of implementing a Talent Management and Succession Planning process this year:

Company Priority #1: _____

Company Priority #2: _____

Company Priority #3: _____

Company Priority #4: _____

Company Priority #5: _____

How will these priorities affect the launch of a new talent management strategy? How can the talent management strategy support and enhance the success of these priorities? Take some time to discuss these priorities and questions with your business and human resource partners, to obtain ideas that will increase the success and business alignment of your talent management strategy.

NOTES:

You may not have the sponsorship of the CEO because it is very difficult for you to meet with him or her to explain or present the program. If this is the case, you are going to need at least one sponsor on the CEO's executive team who can provide the backing and funds you need – an executive sponsor you are able to meet with to present the program and plans.

So, if you are reading this knowing that your CEO is already backing you and is ready to go with the program, you can stop reading and go to the next section. If you are not sure about the sponsorship and support you will be receiving from the CEO, use the forms on the following pages to document the names of other executive and senior level leaders in the company who are already providing the sponsorship you need (and those who are potential future sponsors), and the motivators you can leverage to increase your sponsorship level.

Solid Talent Management Business Leader Sponsors

1. _____

What motivates this leader to sponsor a talent management strategy?

2. _____

What motivates this leader to sponsor a talent management strategy?

3. _____

What motivates this leader to sponsor a talent management strategy?

4. _____

What motivates this leader to sponsor a talent management strategy?

5. _____

What motivates this leader to sponsor a talent management strategy?

NOTES:

Potential Talent Management Business Leader Sponsors:

1. _____

What could potentially motivate this leader to sponsor a talent management strategy?

2. _____

What could potentially motivate this leader to sponsor a talent management strategy?

3. _____

What could potentially motivate this leader to sponsor a talent management strategy?

Regarding the Potential Sponsors you listed above, what actions do you need to take to develop them into Solid Sponsors? Write your ideas here:

- _____

- _____

- _____

- _____

- _____

Gather Information

In addition to executive level sponsors within your company, you will want external informational resources to help provide ideas, metrics, benchmarking data, and even encouragement. Your external resources may include:

- Formal organizations that provide benchmarking data and metrics on succession planning and talent management, such as the Corporate Leadership Council (CLC), the Learning & Development Roundtable, the American Society of Training and Development (ASTD), and the Society of Human Resource Management (SHRM). Note: These organizations require either individual memberships or organizational members to obtain the benefits and resources they provide.

  NOTE: In addition to providing benchmarking information, articles, seminars, and virtual learning events, the Corporate Leadership Council can also connect you with other members as a networking function, enabling you to talk to other professionals to obtain ideas, best practices, and lessons learned.

- Conduct Internet searches on available articles, conferences, and consultants who specialize in succession planning and talent management.

- Network with any of the leaders in your company who worked at other organizations with a Talent Review or succession planning process to obtain best practice ideas.

Define Your Goals

Now that you've gathered information and identified sponsors, you will want to work with your sponsors to define the goals for your Talent Management Program. Potential goals may include:

- ❏ **Strengthening Your Leadership Pipeline:** Just as your Sales organization works continuously to build a strong potential customer pipeline, one goal of your program may be to build a strong leadership pipeline, starting with individual contributors who are being prepared for leadership roles, to mid-level leaders who are being prepared for broader, more complex roles, to senior leaders who are being prepared for executive roles. Part of this goal may also be to identify under-performing leaders during the Talent Review discussions.

  Your ultimate goal is to have multiple and talented individuals within each part of this pipeline to retain your leaders and to have an internal talent pool to tap into as new leadership positions become available.

- ❏ **Identify, Develop, and Retain High Potential Individuals:** Another goal of your program may be to identify High Potential individuals who are the current top performers and the future high potential leadership talent for your organization.

Your goal is to retain these individuals, and to develop and prepare them for leadership roles.

❑ **Strengthening Customer and Shareholder Perceptions:** Especially in large publicly held organizations, the existence or absence of solid succession planning processes, especially for executive-level positions, can play a part in the perception of Wall Street, and of potential customers, regarding the long-term leadership strength of the organization.

Some large organizations have suffered poor publicity (and lost value through stock drops or lawsuits) due to problems within their internal succession planning and executive development preparations. Other companies are known for the strength of their leadership development programs and processes, which adds to their credibility and perception of long-term viability.

❑ **Reducing External Recruiting Costs:** The cost of using external recruiting firms for most or all of your leadership positions can be staggering. Certainly you will always want to bring in "fresh leadership talent" for some positions, but if this is done excessively, then the "hard" cost of external recruitment fees and the "softer" costs associated with the lack of leadership consistency are definitely not assets to the company.

In addition, an organization that recruits for leadership positions externally on a regular basis runs a much higher risk of losing their best internal talent, who see that they have little or no chance of long-term career growth within the organization. Finally, there is a cost related to a longer transition time and initial learning curve that is usually associated with external hires that can be reduced by increasing internal hires who are already familiar with the company, the industry, policies, culture, and the internal people network.

❑ **Identifying Development Positions and Leadership Competency Gaps:** As you move through your Talent Review process, you will find some leadership positions in the company that are ideal as "development ground" for leaders to move into. These positions will expose the individual to a critical pool of knowledge or skills that will be needed at the executive level. In addition, you may also find some weak pockets of leadership benchstrength, which can then be handled on a proactive basis, rather than waiting until the issue reaches a more visible and/or crisis state.

❑ **Retain Critical Experts:** As part of your Talent Review process, you may want to identify individuals who demonstrate one or more key competencies at a high level. While everyone is vital in their position, these individuals have a unique and highly complex set of competencies that cannot easily be duplicated. You may want to set a goal to identify and retain these individuals. In addition, you may want to provide additional or special compensation or recognition for these employees, and/or you may want to implement a special development or retention program for them.

❑ **Identify Leadership Position Vacancy Risk:** Another possible goal of your program may be to identify the leadership positions that currently are held by an individual who is perceived to be at a high vacancy risk level. When these individuals are identified, it is important to assess the risk to the organization if they do leave, and to review their current succession plan. It may also be important to identify additional retention measures to be taken to reduce the vacancy risk exposure, such as reviewing their compensation, providing a new development challenge, promoting the individual, recognizing the individual's results and contribution to the company, etc.

❑ **Work Proactively on Leadership Career Movement:** Part of your Talent Review process may be to discuss the next potential career move(s) of each leader, and to identify leaders who have reached the peak of performance and experience in their current role, and are no longer being challenged. Identifying these individuals will provide a way for the internal recruiting process to focus on these individuals for potential new and challenging internal job placements.

Define Your Talent Review Philosophies

Before proceeding with a Talent Review process, there are several decisions that must be made regarding the philosophy and practices your organization intends to follow. The exciting thing about this field of work is that it is very cutting edge and it encourages innovative ideas about how actions should be executed.

At this time, there are very few "clear-cut" best practices or established processes to draw upon. For example, some companies notify individuals that they have been identified as high potentials and others do not. It is a somewhat controversial and newer function of Human Resources. For this reason, it is critical that you and your senior leader sponsors agree on some decisions up front, such as:

- Will we identify a High Potential population as part of our Talent Review process?

- If we identify a High Potential population, will we notify them?

- Will we notify Successors?

- Will we create and provide corporate development programs for High Potentials, or will the managers of these individuals be responsible for developing them?

- Will we provide corporate development programs for Successors, or will the managers of these individuals be responsible for notifying them?

- What metrics will we use to measure our processes and program?

- Will we publish or announce the names of the high potentials and/or successors publicly in the company? **Note:** Very few organizations publicize the names of their high potentials to the entire organization, due to the risk of internal morale issues, as well as the risk of exposing their names to competitors and external recruiters.

- How often will we have Talent Review meetings? How often will we ask the leaders to review and update their succession plans and development actions?

- What quantifiers will we use for Talent Review discussions? What do we want to know and describe each about each leader? Examples include:

  o Strengths

  o Development Areas

  o Position Vacancy Risk

  o Termination Risk

  o Next Potential Career Move (with or without specifying a timeframe)

  o Leadership Stage

  o Length of time in company

  o Length of time in position

  o Learning Agility

  o Relocation Potential / Status

  o Advancement Desire

  o Advancement Ability

  o Employee Engagement Level

  o Career History – Past Career Moves and Experience

  o Number of direct and indirect reports in the leader's organizational structure

  o Education / Certifications / Licenses

  o Recent development actions completed

- If we have a High Potential corporate development program, will participants stay in the program indefinitely? Or will they stay in the program for a specific number of years? Or will they stay in the program one year at a time, to be "re-selected" (or not) each year during the Talent Review process?

- What will be our internal recruiting policy of High Potential individuals? Will High Potentials have any type of preferential or "first look" status for open positions, especially if the open position would be a development step for the individual? Ultimately, who owns the talent in the business units and in the company?

- What is the definition of a High Potential in our company? Will we have multiple categories of High Potentials? Possible high potential categories may include:

  o Manager Trainee High Potentials (employees who are currently individual contributors with demonstrated leadership potential and abilities)

  o New Leadership High Potentials

  o Experienced Leadership High Potentials

  o Executive-level High Potentials

  o Top Global High Potentials

- What is the definition of a Successor? Will we have multiple levels of successors? Possible successor categories include:

  o Temporary Successor – an individual who could cover the position on a temporary basis until a successor fills the position

  o Successor – an individual who is fully qualified to fill the incumbent's position

  o 1-3 Year Successor – an individual who requires additional skills, experience, and/or education, but could be potentially ready as a successor within a few years

  o 4-5 Year Successor – an individual who is demonstrating high potential in the department, but requires 4-5 more years of experience, training, and coaching to be qualified as a prepared successor

- What leadership level will be involved in the Talent Review process? Examples include:

  o What level of leaders will be required to create a succession plan? Executives only? Leaders in director and above positions? All leaders?

  o What level of leaders will be discussed in the Talent Review meeting? Will we discuss all leaders in the business unit? Will we discuss leaders down to the manager level but not the supervisor level? Will we only discuss leaders in Vice President positions and above?

- o What level of leaders will be invited to participate in the Talent Review meeting? (Note: For optimum discussion and timing, an ideal Talent Review meeting group size is 5-10 participants)

- o If we have a High Potential program, will we have a percentage guideline to control the number of participants selected for the program? For example, some companies have a guideline of 1% of the population, others have a guideline of 5%, and other organizations may have a guideline of 10%. The size of the entire organization will affect this decision. If no guideline is established, typically leaders will nominate large percentages of their population for the High Potential program (at least they will until they learn that training these individuals may be costly).

  NOTE: If this is the first time your organization is conducting Talent Review meetings and identifying High Potentials, leaders will often identify too many people as high potentials until the process matures in your company and the definition of a High Potential becomes better understood and established as part of your culture.

- If we have a High Potential program, who will provide the final approval of these individuals? For example, will your CEO want to approve all employees in the population, or just the senior-level High Potentials? Will all Vice Presidential level leaders and above, in each business unit, be required to approve the High Potential individuals?

We recommend that at the very least, your CEO and/or executive team will need to review and approve your top level high potentials – those who are being developed for executive-level or global-level positions in your company. If this does not occur, you risk setting expectations with an individual who is not truly seen as a realistic candidate for the position they are being developed for. In addition, you will spend time and serious funds on developing an individual for an executive-level role he or she will almost certainly never have, if they don't have the sponsorship and credibility at the executive level.

In addition (depending on your organization) you may also need or require approval from your Board of Directors of very top-level executive successor positions. This is especially true if you are working in a publicly traded company.

Prepare Your Organization

Possibly the most important piece of advice you will get from this book is to make sure you have other leadership and professional development programs and resources in place for leaders who are not selected as high potentials when you implement talent management strategies for the first time. These development programs should already be contributing to your culture and business results when you implement the new Talent Review and Succession Planning processes.

First of all, it is important to have leadership development resources for leaders throughout the company because you don't want to create a culture where only the top 1% or 5% of the population receives adequate development opportunities. This could cause both morale and even potential legal problems, and would definitely not provide for the overall career and talent development your organization needs. It would certainly make it difficult to respond to anyone who feels that the high potential program is creating an "elitist" group in the organization, and this is almost certainly one of the concerns leaders in the company will have about the program. You will want to provide the resources to be able to assure both leaders and employees that development and career opportunities are available to all employees in the company.

Secondly, having other development programs and resources in place provides a larger "toolkit" of development suggestions you can provide during the Talent Review process. For example, let's say during the Talent Review meeting you are having with senior leaders, a manager is described as behaving more like an individual contributor. As development ideas, you might suggest on-the-job development actions to address this issue, such as having the business unit leaders identify a mentor in the department for her – someone who is already a strong leader in the department.

Or maybe you learn that this manager has never received feedback on this behavior, so you recommend coaching and a development plan. But also, if you already have development resources and programs in place, you can suggest options such as a 360-feedback process, or a workshop in how to lead more effectively through others.

If you don't already have leadership development resources in place, to some extent your Talent Review process ends up with more problems than solutions identified.

> *If your leaders are comfortable and have the skills to discuss employee performance and leadership readiness, this will certainly make the Talent Review discussions easier, and will result in the rich, productive conversations that are needed for results.*

Additionally, your Talent Review process will be more successful if your culture emphasizes the coaching and development of employees, which typically includes leadership development workshops or other learning resources that are designed to build these skills in your leadership population. If your leaders are comfortable and skilled in discussing employee performance and leadership readiness, this will certainly make the Talent Review conversations run more smooth and will result in the rich, productive discussions that are needed for results.

Identify Adequate Resources

The size and structure of the organizational chart of personnel devoted to the company's Talent Review process, Succession Planning, and Leadership Development varies greatly, from assigning these projects as a part-time initiative to one person in Human Resources, to a full organizational structure that includes leaders and employees responsible for

Executive Development, Talent Management, Succession Management, Career Development, and Leadership Training.

Our recommendation is that you have at least one full-time employee devoted completely to these initiatives, even if your company is in the small to medium range. This is because you will find that the responsibilities of these projects are extensive and these programs require ongoing work throughout the year to be successful.

On the following page you will see a list of sample of typical job responsibilities for individuals with responsibility for Leadership Development and/or Talent Management, which can be used to write job descriptions, job requisitions, proposals for additional personnel, job advertisements, etc.

Talent Management – Potential Job Responsibilities

- Overall Leadership Development Strategy, Program Design, and Management

- Talent Review Process Design and Implementation

- Communication of Strategy and Processes to Leadership Team

- Identify and Implement a 360 Feedback Process and System

- Serve as an internal 360 Feedback Coach and/or Executive Coach

- Facilitate Talent Review Meetings

- Work with Senior Leadership to Identify and Communication Leadership Competencies for the Organization

- Conduct Needs Assessment to Identify Solutions for Leadership Competency Needs

- Implementation of Leadership Development Programs, Workshops, and Resources

- Conduct Evaluations and Calculate Return-On-Investment on Leadership Programs

- Develop and Implement Programs for High Potential Employees

- Lead the High Potential Notification and Communication Process

- Lead the Succession Planning Process – Work with Business Unit Leaders to Identify and Develop Successors

- Implement an Executive Coaching Process (Including an External Vendor or Internal Coaches)

- Implement a Talent Management Process to Obtain High Potential Nominees and Successor Nominees to be Finalized During the Talent Review Meetings

- Identify and Implement E-Learning Resources for Leadership Development

- Identify and Implement a Talent Management and Succession Planning Online System

- Implement a Mentor Program (this may be a mentor program for the general population, or for a specific group – i.e. for women and/or minorities with leadership potential, for a high potential group, etc.)

- Work with Talent Acquisition / Career Development / Recruiting Personnel to Implement Policies and Procedures for Career Movement of High Potentials and Successors

- Work with External Vendors Regarding Contracts, Negotiation of Pricing, Customization of Products, Obtaining Non-Disclosure Agreements, Scheduling of Workshops, etc.

- Implement a Development Program for Executive High Potentials, Including an Executive Assessment Center, Executive Sponsorships, and Development Plans

- Facilitate Leadership Development Workshops, Focus Groups, Presentations, etc.

- Develop and Implement a New Manager Orientation Process and Development Program

- Develop and Implement a Manager Trainee Orientation Process and Development Program

You will also need to create a budget for the Talent Review and Succession Planning process, including the leadership development resources, consultants, and materials needed. Another large potential expenditure is the type of system you will want to use for Talent Management, which you can use during Talent Review meetings to document discussions, and for the storage, tracking, and use of your talent data after the Talent Review meetings have been completed.

Establish Leadership Accountability for People Development

Plan now for the actions you will implement (or that may already be in place) to hold leaders accountable for participation in the Talent Review and Succession Planning process, and especially for the ongoing development actions that will be identified in the Talent Review meetings that will require follow through over the coming year. If there is no incentive or accountability factor involved in your process, you may have some difficulty ensuring that all business units and all leaders will participate and follow through consistently across the company.

Here are some Accountability action items and ideas for your Talent Review and Succession Planning process:

- **The Performance Review** – Within the Performance Review plan for leaders in your company, include an objective for all leaders pertaining to people and leadership development, including the identification of successors, providing both formal and on-the-job training opportunities for employees, hiring and retaining talented employees, ensuring all employees have a written development plan, etc. Make sure the objective has a strong enough percentage weight to create a significant contribution to the overall performance review rating.

- **Executive Support and Communications** – As with most Human Resources initiatives, some leaders will jump at the opportunity to schedule and follow through with the Talent Review and Succession Planning process, others will do it but they may have some concerns or questions about the process, and there are normally a few who drag their feet and may stall the completion of the process for the entire organization. This is the point at which you need your executive support to be willing to communicate to the business unit leaders that this is an important company-wide initiative that requires timely follow through.

  Additionally, when annual Talent Review processes are about to begin, accountability is greatly enhanced if the announcement and communication about the launch of the process comes from your CEO or executive level Human Resources leader.

- **Business Unit Human Resource or Organizational Development Partners** – Any Human Resource personnel who are partnered with your business units can conduct at least quarterly or mid-year "mini-Talent Review" sessions that require the senior leadership teams to discuss progress on the development gaps and actions identified during the Talent Review process. This is also a good time for leaders to update their Succession Plans, as these will change during the year as new employees enter the company and as employees leave the company or make internal career moves.

- **Provide Recognition, Opportunity, and/or Financial Rewards** – Organizations that are most successful at making employee development an important part of their culture are the organizations that recognize and reward leaders who develop their employees.

  Some companies find it works well to align their talent management goals with merit and compensation rewards, such as including the leader's talent management actions into the calculation used for bonuses. For example, the bonus calculation could include metrics such as:

  - ✓ The completion of a business unit's Talent Review meeting

  - ✓ Completed succession plans for specified levels of leadership

✓ Completed career and development plans for all employees

✓ 100% participation level of all new leaders in the business unit completing a new management training program

✓ 100% completion of the performance review process

Another way to recognize leaders who develop their employees is to spotlight them in the company newsletter, citing percentages such as the employees who experience career advancement in the group annually, or highlighting the business unit as a case study in application of development actions, or demonstrating the enhanced business results the group has achieved by applying a newly trained skill, knowledge, or process on the job.

- **Provide Reports and Metrics to Senior Leaders** – Providing development progress data in report format (i.e. percentage of Talent Review action plans completed, percentage of new leaders completing the company's new management trainee program) can also be effective in holding leaders accountable for development follow through actions.

  In addition, providing return-on-investment data for business units regarding either expenses saved or increased profits will make a significant difference in the value your business units see in the Talent Review process, and the accountability they will demonstrate through their own participation and follow through.

  If your company has any type of "Metrics Dashboard", make sure at least one metric regarding the growth and development of your leadership benchstrength is included, to increase the accountability and significance of the Talent Review and Succession Planning process within the organization.

- **Organizational Talent Review or Executive Steering Committee** – Another idea for creating increased accountability for leadership development is to create an ongoing "governing body" that is designed to oversee the process, the results, and the ongoing improvements needed to continually increase the effectiveness of the process. This forum may be an Organizational Talent Review meeting, held at least annually (quarterly or semi-annually would be more effective) to review the overall organizational results of all business unit Talent Reviews. This places accountability on the business unit leaders to ensure they are ready to present their talent and development actions to the executive team.

  Another type of governing body is a Talent Management Steering Committee (or Talent Council), composed of senior level business unit leaders and human resource leaders. This committee would have responsibility for high level talent management (i.e. review of potential internal candidates and successors for an open Vice President level position), as well as for sponsoring Executive High Potentials and monitoring their development plans, and reviewing the results and ongoing progress of the Talent Review actions for each business unit.

- **Provide Real-Time Data and Automation to Leaders** – Leaders needs access to Talent Management data to enable them to view the succession plans within their reporting structure, development plans, competency models and skill gaps, high potential profiles, and potential future candidates for leadership roles. An automated system of this type puts more control and usability of the data in the hands of the leaders, increasing their ability and accountability to keep the data current and to monitor progress within the leadership structure of his or her business unit.

- **Provide Time for Culture Change** – Finally, it is important to realize that making the Talent Review process and focus on Leadership Development part of your company's culture will take time. In the first year of your program, you will be doing <u>very</u> well if all business units just participate in the process and see the value in it. In following years, the leaders will begin to feel more comfortable with the process. They will begin to proactively request the service, and they will trust the process more. You will then see consistent leadership participation and the follow through of action plans will increase as well.

The Next Step – Complete Checklists

Now that you have completed Chapter One: Are You Ready?, take some time to work with your peers and sponsors to review, discuss, and complete the Readiness Checklist. Use this tool to identify the strengths, or driving forces that will provide the support you will need to create an effective program, and the weak spots, or potential restraining forces that could result in roadblocks. Once these potential obstacles are identified, you will want to create contingency plans for them to reduce the risk of these issues.

Finalize Your Plans

After completing the checklists, use the Project Plan Summary section at the end of this book to begin to compile the results of your checklist decisions, and to create an overall project plan that you can use to communicate and execute your strategy.

Readiness Checklist

(The Readiness Checklist offers a chance to test the water before diving in.)

Use the rating scale below to identify your company's strengths and potential weak spots as readiness factors for implementing a succession planning and talent management process. You may not be able to rate all of these factors yet, but they should all be considered before implementation.

Don't be discouraged if several factors are not in place – you can still implement this process in your company successfully! This readiness review will help you leverage your strengths and prepare for potential weak spots as you plan and execute your process.

Readiness Rating Scale:

Scale: 1=Weak Spot   **2=Neutral**   **3=Strength**

IMPORTANT: In each category, one or more **ANCHORS** have been defined. An anchor is a factor that calls for a rating of "3" to lead to the most successful implementation of your Talent Management processes. The anchors are readiness factors that are most critical to the successful implementation of your new processes.

Use the rating scale below to identify your executive level sponsorship readiness factors. Remember, an **anchor** is a readiness factor that calls for a rating of "3" to lead to the most successful implementation of your Talent Management processes.

Sponsorship

Scale: 1=Weak Spot   2=Neutral   3=Strength

1   2   3

☐ ☐ ☐   **ANCHOR: Our executive team requested (or expressed support for) a talent management and succession planning process.**

☐ ☐ ☐   Our executive leaders focus time, energy, and budget on developing their people (or at least some of them do this well).

☐ ☐ ☐   We have budgeted funds specifically targeted for leadership development.

☐ ☐ ☐   Leaders within the company have been asking for a succession planning and talent management process to be implemented.

☐ ☐ ☐   The goals and expected results (and how they will be measured) of a succession planning and talent management process have been defined.

☐ ☐ ☐   Our executive leadership has communicated the importance and purpose of implementing succession planning and talent management to our leaders.

☐ ☐ ☐   We have identified an external mentor, colleague, or consultant to provide ideas, advice, and/or benchmarking information.

☐ ☐ ☐   The company has defined the leadership positions that are most critical to organizational success, and the competencies that these positions require.

Use the rating scale below to identify your company's readiness factors that pertain to the culture in the organization (it may also be important to review culture differences between company sites that could affect the talent management strategy). Remember, an **<u>anchor</u>** is a readiness factor that calls for a rating of "3" to lead to the most successful implementation of your Talent Management processes.

Culture

Scale: 1=Weak Spot   2=Neutral   3=Strength

1   2   3

☐ ☐ ☐   **ANCHOR: Our leaders are comfortable identifying and discussing superior performers, solid performers, and weak performers.**

☐ ☐ ☐   **ANCHOR: Our organization has identified the most important leadership competencies required for success in our organization, and our leadership development programs align with these competencies.**

☐ ☐ ☐   Our leaders are trained to use effective coaching skills to provide feedback to superior performers, solid performers, and those who are under-performing.

☐ ☐ ☐   We made the decision whether or not to notify high potentials after they have been identified.

☐ ☐ ☐   We made the decision whether to notify successors after they have been identified.

☐ ☐ ☐   We have identified and interviewed any leaders within our organization who have experienced succession planning and/or talent management processes in other companies during their career, to obtain their expectations and ideas.

QUESTION: Are there any differences in culture between different work sites or between different business groups that could affect the implementation of a new talent management strategy? Document your notes below:

Use the rating scale below to identify the readiness factors that pertain to your current human resources organizational structure. Remember, an **anchor** is a readiness factor that calls for a rating of "3" to lead to the most successful implementation of your Talent Management processes.

Human Resource Structure

Scale: 1=Weak Spot   2=Neutral   3=Strength

1   2   3

☐ ☐ ☐   **ANCHOR: We have multiple leadership development resources in place to develop all leaders in our organization.**

☐ ☐ ☐   **ANCHOR: At least one employee has the lead responsibility to plan and execute a succession planning and talent management program.**

☐ ☐ ☐   **ANCHOR: Our leaders are held accountable through a performance review process for leadership abilities and/or people development.**

☐ ☐ ☐   Overall, our managers accurately evaluate work performance and goal results during the performance review period.

☐ ☐ ☐   Overall, our managers address performance issues appropriately and in a timely manner.

☐ ☐ ☐   Our company is accustomed to complying with Human Resources processes, policies, and procedures.

☐ ☐ ☐   We have human resource personnel in place to plan and implement the program across all business units in the organization.

☐ ☐ ☐   We have human resource development personnel to work with leaders to follow through on development action plans identified during the talent assessment and succession planning process.

☐ ☐ ☐   We have budget funds allocated for the people, materials, systems, travel, etc. that are needed to implement a talent management strategy.

Use the rating scale below to identify your company's readiness factors pertaining to metrics that are currently available and metrics that could be added to your talent management strategy. Remember, an **anchor** is a readiness factor that calls for a rating of "3" to lead to the most successful implementation of your Talent Management processes.

Metrics

Scale: 1=Weak Spot   2=Neutral   3=Strength

1   2   3

☐ ☐ ☐   **ANCHOR: We have defined the metrics that will demonstrate achievement of the goals defined for the program.**

☐ ☐ ☐   **ANCHOR: The metrics we have identified align with the organization's business strategy and are designed to demonstrate a return-on-investment for our Talent Management process.**

☐ ☐ ☐   We have researched succession planning and high potential program best practices, measurement methodology, and processes.

☐ ☐ ☐   We have baseline data regarding our internal versus external hire rate for leadership positions.

☐ ☐ ☐   We have measured the percentage of leaders who will be eligible to retire in the next 5 years.

☐ ☐ ☐   We have baseline data regarding the employee and/or leadership turnover in our company.

☐ ☐ ☐   We have baseline data regarding the gender and ethnicity of our employee and leadership population.

☐ ☐ ☐   We have data from our managers defining the typical period of time it takes to bring a new leader "up to speed" in our company.

☐ ☐ ☐   We have baseline data regarding the current career movement rates of our leaders, including promotional and lateral position changes.

☐ ☐ ☐   The executive sponsors of this program understand that metrics will need to be gathered and reviewed for multiple years to fully assess the success of the program.

Use the rating scale below to identify the system and/or tools that are in place or are planned as part of your talent management system strategy. Remember, an **anchor** is a readiness factor that calls for a rating of "3" to lead to the most successful implementation of your Talent Management processes.

Systems

Scale: 1=Weak Spot   2=Neutral   3=Strength

1   2   3

☐ ☐ ☐   **ANCHOR: We are able send communications and documents electronically to all leaders; all leaders have their own computer and e-mail systems to enter talent assessment and succession plan data.**

☐ ☐ ☐   **ANCHOR: We have identified a system or software we will use to track the data that will be obtained through the talent review and succession planning process (this may be a system specifically designed for this purpose or it may be a basic software such as Excel).**

☐ ☐ ☐   Our leaders are accustomed to handling tasks and processes online.

☐ ☐ ☐   The system has been designed or customized to match the talent management strategy and processes.

☐ ☐ ☐   Our human resource partners and business unit leaders will have access to the online talent management data throughout the year.

Readiness Summary

Although there is no "magic formula" we can create to tell you absolutely that you are ready to move ahead with a Talent Review and Succession Planning strategy, you will be able to obtain an idea of your readiness factor by summarizing the results of this checklist, using the tool below:

- There are a total of TEN ANCHORS identified on this Readiness Checklist. How many ANCHORS were you able to rate as a 3? _____ How many anchors were you able to rate as a 2? _____ Did you rate any anchors as a 1? _____

  NOTES:

- Of the ANCHORS that you rated as a 1, how critical are these to your organization's culture? What actions can you take to increase the "readiness factors" of these items?

- Summarize the number and percentage of items you identified as:

  o A Strength (Rating of 3)   _____

  o Neutral (Rating of 2)   _____

  o A Weak Spot (Rating of 1)   _____

- What are your thoughts at this point as you review your overall Readiness Results? What will be key factors that will help drive your Talent Review and Succession Planning process forward, and how can you leverage these strengths? What actions can you take to overcome barriers that you have identified?

Chapter Two

High Potential Strategic Decisions

Out of all of the ideas and information you will take away from this book, this section is one of the most critical if you are planning to include high potential identification as part of your talent management process.

NOTE: The information in this chapter is for learning and development purposes; it is not designed to provide legal advice. Consult with your legal department or attorney to review your high potential identification process.

Once your high potential identification criteria and procedures are established, you will want to use it throughout the company throughout a complete cycle of talent assessment. To make sure the process is as accurate as it can be and it fits the organization, you will need to:

Plan the Process

Obtain Feedback on the Process

Update the Process

Ensure all Key Stakeholders Agree

Finalize the Process

Is it an Art or a Science?

Many people question the accuracy of high potential identification. They wonder how future potential can be identified if it is behavior that has not occurred yet. And how can we predict what future leadership competencies will be needed when organizations and the market change so quickly?

The answer is that we can not ensure 100% accuracy of high potential identification any more than we can ensure 100% accuracy of other business decisions that are made to acquire a new company, or to launch a new product, or to enter a new market segment. Most, if not all business decisions are basically "educated guesses" based on available information from multiple sources, formal assessment instruments, best practice benchmarking, analysis of data, and observations.

The same is true for the assessment of talent, and you want to make sure your process includes these same components. A company would never consider making a business acquisition without completing a due diligence process – we should use the same type of "due diligence" thinking to plan for future leadership needs in the organization.

Talent Selection Criteria

The first step an organization should take to create their high potential assessment and identification process is to choose the selection criteria that addresses the company's current <u>and</u> future leadership needs. Examples of selection criteria include:

- **Past work experience and advancement history**

- **Education**

- **Geographic Mobility**

- **Learning Agility**

- **Prior leadership positions – size and scope of leadership responsibilities**

- **Advancement Potential**

- **Advancement Desire**

- **Assessment of the individual compared to the company's values and leadership competencies**

- **Past performance ratings**

- **Formal leadership assessment instruments**

- **The ability to take risks**

Typically the high potential selection criteria includes factors that relate to past performance, and factors that pertain to the future potential of the employee. But both past performance and future potential should be based on factual or observable data.

For example, geographic mobility should be based on the employee's most recent expressed desire to relocate, rather than assuming or guessing this information. Advancement desire should be based on the individual's demonstrated and expressed desire to advance.

Talk to your organization's business leaders and executives to identify what talent needs are expected for future leaders – consider emerging markets, any new business products or services that are planned, customer expansion plans, acquisition and merger strategy, etc. to evaluate the talent needs.

Talent Assessment Methodology

After the talent selection criteria is determined, the next step is to design the methodology that will be used to identify the high potentials. The methodology you use is important both from an accuracy and legal standpoint.

Consistency in your methodology is critical. The high potential identification criteria and process must be duplicated identically across the organization, to ensure all employees are evaluated in the same way.

Quantitative and Qualitative Assessment Methodology

A comprehensive high potential identification process includes two basic steps:

1. **A quantitative talent assessment process** that occurs initially, to provide an objective method for managers to consider the performance and future potential of each employee, and to discuss their results with their leader to ensure agreement at that level.

2. **A qualitative, face-to-face talent discussion** with the participation of multiple business unit leaders. The purpose of this step is to collect several data points from multiple perspectives, and compare this against the company's leadership competencies.

The Quantitative Step

The importance of the quantitative step is to compare talent within a group, using "apples to apples" criteria, to avoid actual or perceived favoritism from the managers who initially identify individuals as high potentials. This step uses the talent identification criteria that you identified, and it typically involves rating systems or other objective assessment processes. For more information on this talent assessment quantitative step, refer to the Talent Assessment chapter of this book.

As the talent management leader, you will want to have access to these assessment results, to compile and analyze them prior to the next step – the Talent Review meeting.

The Qualitative Step

The qualitative step should include discussions with leaders in the business unit or company who can provide data points they have observed and experienced with each individual, through a Talent Review meeting or process. This could take place as an individual interview process, but a best practice method involves bringing the leaders together to discuss their talent as a group. This is where the "richness" of the data points occurs.

Up to this point, the talent assessment process has only been from the manager's perspective. In this phase of the process there is an opportunity to hear many other perspectives to agree upon and finalize the high potential population. This qualitative step increases the validity of the selection of high potentials and successors by adding a discussion and consensus step to the process.

What Size Will Your High Potential Population Be?

One early decision you will need to make pertains to the size of your high potential population – this will most likely be a specific percentage of your population. Most companies identify between 1% and 5% of their organization for the high potential group.

You will want to have this type of size guideline for business leaders to work within. You'll find that some leaders want to identify around 50% of their work teams as high potential leaders. This is fine during the initial identification and quantitative stage because you want to be inclusive rather than exclusive, and you want to be able to identify many high potentials and high performers who can contribute to a variety of company initiatives. The Talent Review discussions will serve to differentiate the high potentials from the high performers, which will result in a smaller group of confirmed high potentials to participate in a focused development program.

Always keep in mind that the purpose of the high potential exercise is not to "rack 'em and stack 'em", but to assess your human talent against the future leadership needs of the company. So provide a size or percentage guideline to your leaders, but don't rule out "one more" high potential in a group just because the size of their population has already been maxed out.

What Level of Employees Will We Include?

You will also need to work with your business leaders to determine what levels of the population will be considered for high potential nomination. Some companies only have an executive-level high potential population. Others only have managers in their high potential programs, and some companies have employees at multiple levels – from the individual contributor level to the executive level in their high potential program.

This is not a decision that you have to finalize in your first year of implementation. Many companies start both their high potential nomination and succession planning programs at the executive level, and then add additional layers of the organization to this process over time. In fact, this is frequently done to avoid the pitfall of "trying to do it all" in a short period of time.

Your high potential nomination process should correlate to the level of your succession planning process. For example, if you have all directors and above complete succession plans in your company, this means they are assessing talent down through the management level. So your high potential population might be manager level and above employees, because that population is already being evaluated.

Some companies also categorize their high potentials into groups such as "executive potentials" or "new leader potentials". This can be done during the high potential nomination process, but be aware that it can cause confusion for leaders, who can get "hung up" on the category to place the individual in.

Another option is to simplify the nomination process by just working with leaders to identify a high potential population as a whole. Then, the talent management or human resources team can determine the appropriate development category for each individual to ensure they are connected to learning resources that are appropriate for their leadership level.

Will We Identify Low Potentials or Low Performers?

During the quantitative and qualitative talent assessment and review process, you may also be reviewing leaders who require additional special actions to improve performance. For example, you might be identifying employees who are ready for a career move, even if they are not in the high potential group. You may discuss employees who may be at high risk of leaving the company and identifying a retention action plan for them. And, during this time you might also be identifying low performers.

The talent review discussion meeting is an appropriate time to also review low performers and low potentials, to determine an action plan to address the issue. One solution might be to place the individual in a different role that is a better job fit. Another solution might be to have a high performer mentor the low performer, especially if the skill deficiency is on one specific area that can be learned, or if the lower performer is simply new to the job.

Keep in mind that it is realistic and appropriate to expect that a need for a formal performance improvement action may surface during the meeting. We've been in meetings where a performance issue of a specific employee is discussed for the first time out in the open among the senior leadership team.

Identifying Critical Experts

In addition to identifying high potential employees for leadership roles in the organization, some companies also identify employees who are critical to the business primarily because of a unique area of expertise that they provide. These individuals demonstrate competencies that are very complex – competencies that take many years to develop. Typically, these employees possess strong technical knowledge, as well as strong knowledge of the organization's industry.

For example, a telecommunications company may want to identify and recognize critical research and development engineers who have designed new (and patented) products for the company, who are recognized both in their field and in the industry as experts.

The follow-up actions for these individuals may be different than the actions initiated for high potential employees. The company may provide a greater compensation or retention package for these individuals. They may ask these critical experts to mentor others in the organization, or to provide special presentations or training workshops to others.

Your organization should consider if this is an appropriate action to take, either as part of your Talent Assessment and Talent Review process, or as a separate program. Having a Critical Expert program in the company also sends the message that employees who either do not wish to become leaders, or who do not demonstrate strong leadership characteristics, also have a key role in the organization that is recognized for the significant value they bring to the success of the company.

Other Talent Management Policy Decisions

Once high potentials and successors have been identified on your organization, your organization will need to agree on internal recruiting policies concerning these individuals.

For example, will high potentials be given first priority for open positions? If a high potential is interested in a new position in the company (or if another leader is interested in having a specific high potential employee for the job), and the leader of this high potential can not spare him or her without a significant business impact, how will this decision be made? Who will have access to the "high potential list" in your company, whether this is a partial list or a full list? What will the process be in the company to obtain succession planning data when a leadership position becomes vacant?

Ideally, it is best to discuss and create these policy decisions in the earlier planning phase of your Talent Management implementation.

Final Key Thoughts

Be sure that everyone involved in the high potential process agrees on why they are doing this. Why are we identifying high potentials, and what are we going to do with them after we've identified them? How will we develop these individuals? If this identification process is not planned carefully and executed effectively, it can hurt morale and cause potential legal problems.

After you are clear on your purpose, relax and remember you can tackle this in "bite-size" pieces; for example, your initial high potential group may be small and easily managed, and over time you can continue to increase the size of the population and the development resources you provide to the high potential group.

Checkpoint: Summarizing High Potential Goals

Use this section to summarize your thoughts from this chapter regarding the goals you want to implement for your high potential identification goals.

Ratings: 1 = Part of our current strategy

2 = Part of our future strategy

3 = Not Applicable or To Be Determined

1   2   3

☐ ☐ ☐   We will identify individuals as "high potential" during our leadership talent review process.

☐ ☐ ☐   We will identify approximately ____% of the organization as high potential (enter the percentage of the organization you plan to identify as high potential; i.e. 1%, 5%, 10%, etc.)

☐ ☐ ☐   We will identify high potentials at the executive level in the organization.

☐ ☐ ☐   We will identify high potentials who are already in leadership positions who could advance quickly into higher level, broader, and more complex leadership positions.

☐ ☐ ☐   We will identify high potentials who are still in an individual contributor role, to proactively develop them for future leadership positions.

☐ ☐ ☐   We will identify top individuals who could move globally into leadership positions within various geographic regions.

☐ ☐ ☐   We will use an executive assessment center to select executive high potentials.

☐ ☐ ☐   We will identify individuals in the organization who are critical to retain for their unique competencies rather than for their leadership skills.

☐ ☐ ☐   We will provide opportunities for our critical experts to teach and mentor others in the organization in their area of expertise.

☐ ☐ ☐   We will provide special compensation or financial retention rewards to those who have been identified as critical experts.

☐ ☐ ☐   We need to review our internal recruiting policies to factor in our new Talent Management strategy.

Chapter Three

Succession Planning Strategic Decisions

Succession Planning is the practice of identifying individuals who can fill specific leadership roles in the future. Incumbent leaders may currently occupy these roles, or they may be new leadership roles that are planned for the future.

The terms "succession management" and "replacement planning" may also be used to label this practice. Typically, replacement planning is considered to be the simplest form of succession planning, in which leadership roles with incumbents who are expected to retire or move on to other roles are reviewed to determine who will be ready to take their place at that time.

However, it is important to note that replacement planning may be a solid first step as an organization implements a talent management strategy for the first time. Over time, replacement planning can evolve into a more robust succession management strategy.

Succession management is usually considered to be a more "robust" exercise which includes replacement planning, but also includes activities such as defining a development plan for each successor, identifying competency gaps successors need to develop to be prepared to move into the role they have been identified for, and identifying successors for future leadership roles that will be needed.

Talent Pools

There are many times that it makes more sense to identify a "pool" of individuals to develop for a specific job title, rather than identifying specific successors to replace one leader.

For example, let's say that Lauren Taylor is one of six Vice Presidents of Finance in the company, who all have similar roles but support different business units. Rather than creating a separate succession plan for her and for each of the Vice Presidents of Finance, you could identify a talent pool of people to prepare to fill any of the six Vice President of Finance positions. This is a much more effective and proactive succession planning method when you have multiple leaders occupying similar positions in the company.

Succession Planning Decisions

If this is the first year you are implementing a succession planning process in your company, there are several things to think about as you are planning your strategy:

- What level of leaders will create succession plans? Will all leaders participate in the succession planning exercise, or will we just begin with executive-level succession plans?

- What level of succession plans will we discuss during the Talent Review meetings? Will we discuss all succession plans that are created in the company or just the succession plans for high level leadership positions?

- If applicable, what does our Board of Directors expect to see from our succession planning results?

- Will any of our current or prospective customers or business partners ask about our succession plans, and if so, what information will we have ready for them?

- Who in the company will be able to view succession plan information once it is finalized?

When you are thinking about these questions, the important thing to keep at the forefront is the purpose of your succession planning process. For example, if the primary catalyst for the implementation of your succession planning initiative is weak bench strength in your leadership population, it will be critical to make sure your succession planning process includes supervisors, managers, and even team leads or other individual contributors who are not yet in leadership positions.

But if your primary goal is to develop ncw cxecutive-level leaders for an expanding customer base or a new product line, you would not want to focus your time on the supervisor-level succession plans, which would likely be very time consuming.

This is another place where it is important not to "bite off more than you can chew" at one time. Factor in the resources and staff you have to lead and implement your succession planning process.

If you have a full talent management staff, you may be able to complete a succession planning process with every leader in the company. If this just one item on your already full workload plate, you may want to just focus on the senior leadership of the company, where the ROI is most obvious through the reduction of executive search fees when you have internal leaders who are prepared to step into high visibility roles.

When thinking about who to share succession plan information with, you will most likely want to share the information with at least the senior business leaders, human resource personnel, and appropriate internal recruiters.

It will be important to make sure the information is provided to the appropriate people in a confidential manner; you definitely don't want the information to leak out to your competitors or external recruiters. But also remember that it does not make sense to go through all of the time and energy it takes to build succession plans only to hold it close to you.

One way to balance the confidentiality issue while you are sharing the information with others is to provide the portion of the data that is applicable to the individual. For example, the Human Resources manager who supports the Sales department may only need succession plan information for the Sales department, and for related departments with potential cross-functional successors.

Successor Categories

Most companies create "readiness" categories for successors to indicate whether the successor is already qualified to fill the incumbent's position, or if the successor will be ready in a projected number of years in the future.

To help leaders decide if a successor should be in the "ready now" category, ask the leadership team if they would interview the individual as a qualified candidate if the incumbent's position became open today. If the answer is "no", then ask the leaders what work experience, behavioral, and/or educational gaps exist that prevent the individual from being a qualified candidate at this time. Use this information to build development plans for your future successors.

The Identification Process

Like the identification of high potentials, a 2-step process works well for the identification of successors:

1. Communicate the succession planning process and definitions to your leaders; ask them to complete their own succession plans on their own first, and to discuss them with their own leader for initial consensus.

2. Compile the business unit succession plans and provide this document to your business unit leaders in a face-to-face leadership team meeting.

During the succession plan discussion, meeting participants will think of additional potential successors, and they may "move people around" on the succession plan.

> *Typically, the original business unit succession plan will change significantly and increase in validity during the face-to-face discussion and consensus meeting to finalize the plans.*

Identification of Key Leadership Roles

To further enhance the effectiveness of your succession plans, work with your business leaders to identify the key positions in business unit. During this exercise, think of the job itself, not the person who is currently filling the position. Identifying the most business critical positions in the business unit enables the company to:

- Place high potential or high performer talent in these roles

- Focus proactive talent sourcing efforts on these positions before they become open, to ensure successors or talent pools are being developed

- To focus urgent recruiting efforts on the position if it becomes vacant

As you are working with leaders to identify key roles, think about:

- The positions that would be the "last to go" if the company experienced a reduction in positions

- The positions that are most closely aligned with critical business goals

- The positions that would cause the biggest financial impact if they became vacant, resulting in lost opportunities or other significant costs

Your Succession Plan – A Living Document

Succession plans should be discussed and updated on a regular basis by leaders in each business group. The following ideas can help your organization develop successors and increase your leadership benchstrength:

- ❑ Work with leaders to ensure succession plan discussions and updates at least on a quarterly or 6-month basis; the most important part of these discussions is to review the documented development actions and progress for successors, to increase the leaders' accountability toward following through with development activities with these employees

- ❑ Include the development of successors in each leader's performance review goals

- ❑ Provide metrics to senior leaders regarding the identification of successors, the development of successors, and job fills by successors within their business units

- ❑ Develop procedures within your organization's Recruiting or Talent Management function for using successors and high potential candidates for replacement and newly created jobs

- ❑ Develop reward and recognition systems for leaders who demonstrate strong success in the areas of people development and succession planning

- ❑ Implement one of the variety of succession planning systems available to help you document, monitor, and measure your succession plans

- ❑ Identify successors who are not already in another formal development program or plan (i.e. successors who are not also in the high potential program or other formal leadership development program); work with the leaders of these successors to help create a development plan for these successors

❑ For individuals who have been notified of their succession plan status, provide opportunities for increased networking and/or formal interviews with the leadership team of the business unit and the company

❑ Successors at the executive level will need additional development through actions such as job rotations, additional profit and loss responsibility, a special assignment working a challenging project or situation, additional exposure to board members, financial analysts, customers, etc.

The primary keys to creating and maintaining a succession plan that yields prepared leaders and business results are to continuously review and update the plans, and to hold leaders accountable for succession planning and the development of successors. Succession management will yield business results such as increased internal hiring for leadership positions, reduced recruiting costs, and increased leadership benchstrength, retention and readiness for future leadership positions.

Checkpoint: Summarizing Succession Planning Goals

Use this section to summarize your thoughts from this chapter regarding the goals you want to implement for your succession planning initiative.

Ratings: 1 = Part of our current strategy

            2 = Part of our future strategy

            3 = Not Applicable or To Be Determined

1   2   3

☐ ☐ ☐   We will identify individuals who could handle an incumbent leader's position on a temporary, emergency basis if needed.

☐ ☐ ☐   We will identify individuals who are fully qualified to fill the incumbent leader's position if it becomes available.

☐ ☐ ☐   We will identify individuals who could be qualified in 1-3 years to fill the incumbent leader's position if it becomes available.

☐ ☐ ☐   We will identify individuals who could be qualified in 3 or more years in the future to fill the incumbent leader's position if it becomes available.

☐ ☐ ☐   For successors who are not already fully qualified for the incumbent's position, we will identify the competency and/or educational gaps that need to be developed for the successors to become fully prepared.

☐ ☐ ☐   For successors who are not already fully qualified for the incumbent's position, we will work with managers to ensure action takes place to develop the competency gaps for the successors to become fully prepared.

☐ ☐ ☐   We have determined the leadership level in the organization that will create succession plans (i.e. all leaders from the CEO down to the Vice President level will create succession plans). The level we have identified is: _____. In Talent Review meetings, we will discuss the succession plans of these leadership levels: _____.

☐ ☐ ☐   Not only will we identify successors to fill current leadership positions, we will also identify new leadership positions that will be needed in the future, and identify potential successors for these jobs.

☐ ☐ ☐   We will implement communications and processes to encourage leaders to identify potential successors from other work groups, outside of their own reporting structure.

Summarizing Succession Planning Goals (Continued)

Ratings: 1 = Part of our current strategy

2 = Part of our future strategy

3 = Not Applicable or To Be Determined

1   2   3

☐ ☐ ☐ Once the initial succession plans are in place, leaders will be led through an update discussion process on a semi-annual (or quarterly) basis to determine if changes to the plans are needed, and to review development progress of future successors.

☐ ☐ ☐ We will use specific and agreed-upon metrics to measure the results of our succession planning process, such as: _____

_____

☐ ☐ ☐ We will identify potential successors outside of our organization for key leadership positions, and form a plan to proactively recruit these individuals.

☐ ☐ ☐ We will present high-level succession planning results to our executives.

☐ ☐ ☐ We will present executive-level succession plans to our Board of Directors.

Chapter Four

To Tell or Not to Tell, That is the Question

The question of "To tell or not to tell" individuals that they have been identified as high potentials or successors in the company is one of the most controversial questions that talent management professionals wrestle with. The purpose of this chapter is to help you identify the best answer to this question for your organization. We've placed this chapter here in the Planning Section of the book because it is best for the organization to agree on this decision early in the strategy phase of the initiative.

Also, this chapter has been included in this "Planning Stage" section of this book because it is important to collaborate with others on this issue within your organization, and to agree on a decision at this point of the project. Some companies may even delay or cancel the implementation of this type of program because the leaders or sponsors of the program cannot agree on this decision.

In fact, currently there is not a definitive "best practice" regarding this question. Some organizations have a clear policy that high potentials will not be told of their selection in this category, and they depend on their managers to provide additional leadership development.

Some organizations notify the high potentials so they can participate in special development and/or job assignment programs designed specifically for them. Other organizations really never make a clear decision or policy, leaving it up to the discretion of the managers.

High Potential Notification: You Have Choices!

When discussing the question of whether your organization will notify high potentials, remember that you have several different choices within this seemingly "cut and dry" question. Some of these are more controversial and others are more conservative. Here are some examples of the variations on the notification decision that organizations use:

- Employees are identified as "A", "B" or "C" – <u>all employees</u> know their "talent status" in the organization

- <u>Only high potentials are notified</u> by their leaders that they have been identified for this program; the results of the talent assessment process are not discussed with other employees

- High potential employees are not notified that they have been selected for the program; however, <u>the managers of the high potentials are notified</u> and expected to provide special development and/or job assignments to develop their high potential employees

53

- The talent assessment and high potential identification process occurs but <u>no one is notified of the final results</u>; the purpose of the process focuses on increasing the visibility of leadership talent rather than on the development of high potentials

So how does a company decide which of these notification options is the best one for them? One factor to consider is whether the company has an inclusive or exclusive culture. If the company is inclusive in their development, meaning that they have multiple types of development programs to meet a variety of employee levels and needs, notifying and developing high potentials is more likely to be embraced in the company as one more level of their entire development portfolio.

Other factors to consider include the maturity of the organization, the company culture and environment, the ability to give performance feedback, and a company's approach to employee development. If the company does not have other formal development programs, and if the leaders are not skilled at giving performance feedback, notifying high potentials may not work initially.

A company might also take the position not to notify high potentials the first year the program is launched, but to use the first year as an exercise for leaders to move towards a talent mindset, and then notify and develop the high potentials at a later point.

Notifying Successors

As a general strategy, most organizations do not tell individuals they have been identified as a successor for a specific position or person. Unlike the high potential talent pool, successors are being prepared for one or more specific positions, whereas the high potentials are simply receiving greater visibility and development for future leadership roles.

Therefore, successors are generally notified to reduce problems with individuals perceiving they have been "promised" a promotion, or thinking that they are guaranteed to move into the incumbent's position in the future. As everyone in the field of Human Resources knows, there are no promises or guarantees of promotions or of employment, but we also know that employees could perceive that a promise has been made if they are told that they are the successor to Jeremy Spencer's position in the company.

In addition, the development needs of successors are often very specific to the skills needed for the incumbent's position, whereas high potentials can be developed in a broader way to increase their leadership skills, interpersonal competencies, and business acumen, in order to accelerate their preparation for future leadership roles.

Therefore, while high potentials can be notified that they have been selected to participate in a special leadership development program and they can attend development activities together, successors are often developed by the incumbent of the position, because the incumbent knows the unique competencies needed for the job.

When Should Successors Be Notified?

There are situations in which it may be in the best interest of the company to notify one or more successors. Notifying successors is most important and successful when:

- The incumbent has made it known that he/she will be leaving the company within a specified period of time. In this situation, especially at the executive level (and within a publicly held company), the best plan is to notify multiple potential leaders that they are a potential successor to the position, to begin highly focused development actions for each individual.

- The notification process includes verbal and/or written statements making it clear that an individual's succession plan status is not a guarantee of promotion or employment.

- The potential successors have already demonstrated solid professional maturity, and by notifying the successor(s), development of the individual for the incumbent's position will be enhanced and accelerated.

The Advantages of Notifying High Potentials

There are several business advantages associated with notifying individuals that they have been selected to participate in a high potential program. Implementing a notification strategy enables you to directly develop high potentials, place them in key roles and on important customer projects, and measure the program's results.

Typically the high potential population will only be 1% - 5% of your organization. We see no advantage to notifying the other 95% to 99% of your company that they were not selected as a high potential. However, it is critical to provide multiple leadership development resources and programs for this vast majority of leaders in the organization who are not currently being developed within the high potential program.

The advantages of notifying individuals that they have been selected as high potentials are clear:

1. **The Retention Benefit**: These individuals are your top talent and your future leaders for the organization, so you definitely want to let them know how valued they are to increase their retention with the organization. High potentials are more likely than other employees to be recruited frequently, and to be impatient for internal career advancement, so you may already be at a higher risk of losing these talented individuals to your competition.

   When an individual knows they have been identified as a high potential, and they learn they will receive special development, a higher level of visibility in the organization, and potentially more career opportunities, this will almost certainly be a factor in retention and engagement in your company. You can (and should) measure this, by comparing the retention of the high potential population to the comparable overall population in your company. And, we have been told personally multiple times by high potentials that they were considering a career move outside of the company, until they learned that they had been selected as a high potential.

2. **The Development Benefit:** As noted earlier, companies who decide not to notify high potentials typically depend on their leaders to provide additional development to these individuals. Having managers of high potentials involved in the development plan and program for each individual is certainly beneficial, and we definitely recommend that managers have this level of involvement. But if the development program stops there, the program risks losing the ability to:

   ❑ Ensure high potentials are participating in a consistent development program designed to provide learning and job rotational assignments that are aligned with specific leadership competencies, as defined for the organization.

   ❑ Provide the networking and relationship building between the high potential employees. Consider over the years, as these high potentials grow in their careers in the company, how valuable strong cross-functional relationships will be at the senior level in the organization to drive new business opportunities to achieve higher business impact.

   ❑ Use the professional learning and development resources and personnel available to lead and guide the high potentials in their development plan.

And what happens to the high potential employees whose managers leave the company, or the high potentials who may have multiple managers in any given year, due to reorganizations, turnover, and mergers? How will the organization ensure the development of the high potential individual is able to continue in these scenarios?

3. **The Measurement Benefit:** Without a formal development program, it is more difficult to measure the overall business results of the initiative. And, if the organization is able to measure the results, it may be difficult to pinpoint what aspects of the development program are working well, and what needs to be improved, as each manager of each high potential may be handling the development of the employee differently or inconsistently.

High Potential Notification Concerns

So with all of the benefits achieved by notifying high potential employees, why do many companies decide not to notify? The chart on the next page defines the concerns that are usually expressed by organizations with a non-notification policy. These are all very legitimate and very real concerns, and you will most likely need to be able to address these in your company.

Risks and Concerns
Creating an Elitist Group: We will create an elitist group in our organization, or a group who is considered to be the "favorites", if we notify high potentials.
Risk of Lowering Morale and Retention: We risk lowering the morale and engagement level of important, high performing employees; they may even leave the company if they are not selected for the program.
Organizational Concern Over Advancement Opportunity: Employees might think if they are not selected for the program, they will not have opportunities for development and advancement, which could also lower productivity and retention.
The "Big Head" Concern: If we start telling people they are high potentials, they'll get a "big head" over it and become conceited, rather than being team players.
Things Change: Employee performance and potential are subjective and can also change over time – what if we have to tell someone they are no longer in the high potential program?
A Program of "Favored Ones": This concern relates to both the perception and reality of the validity of your high potential selection process. Leaders and employees may perceive the selection process provides a way for leaders to identify their "favorites" for development and advancement opportunities, rather than having a selection process based on merit and potential.
Coaching Avoidance: It will be difficult to explain to employees who are not selected for the program why they were not selected.
Cross-Functional Employee Loss: If others in the organization know who my high potential employees are, they will recruit them into their department, and I will lose my top talent.
Legal Concerns: Employees who are not selected could instigate litigation, citing an unfair selection process, loss of advancement opportunity, etc. Or, employees who are selected may perceive the program as a guarantee of position, employment, or advancement, which could result in a legal problem at some point.

Addressing Risks and Concerns

There are actions you can take to help alleviate all of these concerns. This is not to say that once you put these actions into place that you will never hear about these issues again. The five key suggestions described on the following pages will help you answer questions that leaders will pose to you about your high potential program, and they will reduce the risks of employees who are not selected (or those who are removed from the program) becoming disengaged and disillusioned with the program and the organization.

1. **Provide multiple leadership development and advancement paths and programs.** This is the most important thing to do to alleviate many of the concerns above – make sure the high potential program is not the only leadership development program available to employees. Don't implement a high potential leadership development program unless you have other development options in place that employees can "self-select" for.

   Ideas for leadership programs of this type include a program for newly promoted and/or newly hired leaders, and workshops and programs for senior leaders to enable to them to network and learn with others at their level. Provide the 360-feedback process to any leader – not just to the high potential leaders. This will alleviate concerns about developing an "elitist group", because development and advancement opportunities will be available to all leaders.

2. **Use consistent policies and high potential definitions.** Make sure all Talent Review facilitators, Human Resource managers, and others who represent (or answer questions about) your high potential programs are all using the same "language" when talking with leaders and employees about the high potential program. All of these representatives should clearly understand and be able to articulate the company's definition of a high potential, and should have the ability to consistently answer "tough" questions they may receive on this topic.

3. **Ensure your high potential assessment and selection process is "multi-faceted".** The selection process for the high potential program should include multiple assessment methods and multiple assessors. Implementing a process in which high potentials are selected solely by their own leaders creates the perception (and potentially the reality) that the program is for the "favored ones", and also increases the risk of morale and legal problems.

   Designing a selection process that includes a quantitative component, and a qualitative discussion component (such as a Talent Review meeting) is another critical method of alleviating several of the risks and concerns.

4. **Document the high potential selection and removal process.** To help reduce legal concerns, and to help you address any questions that may come up later about the high potentials who were selected (or those who were removed from the program), make sure you have documentation on:

   ❑ The quantitative assessment process – how were employees rated? Could you thoroughly explain and defend the talent assessment process in court if needed? Was the assessment process implemented in a consistent way in each business unit?

❏ The qualitative assessment process – who were the attendees of the Talent Review meeting? When did Talent Review meetings take place for each business unit? Retain notes from the Talent Review meeting.

❏ The removal process – what is the reason the high potential is being removed from the program? Design a simple form for leaders to document the reason(s) for the removal, and to sign and date this decision.

5. **Provide coaching assistance and "talking points" to leaders.** One reason some companies choose not to notify high potentials pertains to concern about having to answer questions employees may pose about how the company's high potential identification process works. These conversations are not unique to high potential program issues. For example, these questions also occur when promotions take place and more than one employee was interested in the promotion.

As part of the high potential notification process, provide a document of "talking points" for leaders. This is a document that provides information about the program, as well as answers to questions that leaders are likely to receive from employees. Talking Points documents also help ensure more consistent communication about the program from the leaders around the company to their employee groups.

Answers to Difficult Questions

While these five suggestions will help ensure your selection and notification process is as objective, as fair, and as consistent as possible (which is the best way to alleviate the concerns leaders will have about the program), these don't answer all of the questions you may receive about your talent management program. Here are some additional questions and answers that may be helpful:

Question: Why would I want to identify one of my best employees as a high potential? Then I'll lose him or her to another business unit.

Answer: It is true that identifying a very talented employee as a high potential will increase the likelihood that the employee will advance into another work group or department. But high potential employees are more likely to move elsewhere for advancement anyway – identifying and developing them within the company is one of the best ways to retain them, and to build the leadership benchstrength of the company as a whole. It is important to look at the benefits the high potential program provides at an overall company level, rather than at a work team or business unit level.

In addition, most successful top executives have served as a leader in multiple business units, gaining experience in departments such as Operations, Finance, Human Resources, Sales, etc. before moving into high-level positions. Therefore, it is a goal of the program to encourage and assist high potential employees to move cross-functionally in their leadership career, as part of their development program.

Question: How are you going to keep these high potential employees from getting a "big head"?

Answer: This is a concern that leaders sometimes have that, in our experience, does not have a lot of basis in reality. First of all, if the selection process has been done well, the employees selected for the program should have a solid professional maturity and appropriate confidence level, and this type of program will not change that. We have found that employees or leaders who are perceived as being arrogant tend not to be selected by their senior leadership team as a high potential, which "weeds out" potential "big heads" in the first place.

Secondly, provide a "Kickoff Session" (described in detail in this book) for high potential employees as they begin the program, to ensure they hear the message about the confidentiality of their participation in the program, and how to handle any questions they may receive about being in the high potential program.

As project leads and facilitators of high potential programs, we have not seen this to be a big issue, although we have certainly heard people worry about it if they have not experienced high potential identification and development programs previously in their careers.

Much more often than the "big head" syndrome, we've seen the "high potential guilt" syndrome, where high potential employees feel guilty that they were selected over others whom they see as being equally as deserving to be selected for the program.

Question: But things change all of the time. Maybe an employee is seen this year as a high potential, but then the leadership needs and values change, and then the employee is not seen as a high potential, and we'll have to remove them from the program. Is this program worth this risk?

Answer: It is true that leadership needs and values change over time, and the leaders of one group may view an employee as a high potential, and the same employee may not be perceived this way when he or she moves to another business unit.

The best way to combat this problem is to address this issue during the selection process and the initial "Kickoff Session" the high potentials will attend, to introduce them to the program. While of course you will be communicating the value and benefits of the program to the high potentials and to their leaders, make sure you also communicate that individuals may be removed from the program at any time, for a variety of reasons that may or may not pertain at all to the employee's performance or potential.

The key is to make sure your "rules" are clear up front regarding the length of time employees are expected to participate in the program, and whether they will need to be "re-confirmed" each year.

Question: This all seems so subjective and risky – how can you really measure someone's future potential? This means you are trying to measure something that hasn't even occurred yet.

Answer: Every business decision the company makes is a matter of gathering information and making the most informed decision possible, with a level of risk with each decision. There is a level of subjectivity with all other business choices, just as there is with the high potential program.

However, we have learned through research and benchmarking processes that these types of high potential and succession planning processes are considered to be best practices that increase business results, and so like other business decisions we make, we have determined that the benefits of the program outweigh the risk.

While there is a subjective component to trying to measure someone's future potential that has occurred yet, companies take action on a regular basis to determine future potential in other business functions. For example, what is the future potential of this new product or service? What is the future potential of the next potential client? Implementing a solid talent assessment and high potential identification process is another business procedure used to focus on (and measure) the most important resource in the company – the unique talent that is the differentiating feature of each organization.

For example, we are trying to determine future potential of employees before we hire them. We try to determine the future value of a vendor's product or service before we make a purchase. We try to determine the profitability of a new business venture before it is launched. Just like many other aspects of our business, there is both a science and an art to identifying high potential employees.

The subjective component of the selection process is also reduced as much as possible by having multiple assessment criteria, consistent definitions, multiple selectors of high potentials, and using past performance and behaviors, which can be measured, as a predictor of future performance.

Question: What should I say to an employee who asks why he or she was not selected for the high potential program?

Answer: First, it is important to emphasize that new employees will be selected each year (or whatever the Talent Review interval is in your organization), and it is important to focus on positive actions to take towards this goal, if this is the employee's goal.

During this discussion, coach the employee on the leadership strengths he or she already demonstrates, and discuss how these strengths can be leveraged even more – can the employee use these strengths on an upcoming project team? Can the strengths be used in such a way as to increase the visibility of the strength? What development areas may be holding the employee back from being selected for the program? What actions can the employee take to address these development areas?

Question: I have a small work group, and even though I know we won't be announcing who the high potentials are, they'll see the high potentials attending development workshops. This will lower morale in my group overall. How does the value of the high potential program outweigh the morale risk for my entire work group?

Answer: This is a very real and valid concern. First, the most important thing you can do is ensure that everyone in your work group is able to participate in development workshops and/or obtain development resources that meet their needs; make sure the high potentials are not the only ones "going off to workshops". Talk with all of your employees about their career interests, and work with each employee to put together a development plan.

If you as a leader are approached with the question, "Why wasn't I selected for the high potential program?" treat the question in much the same way that you would if the question were "Why didn't I get the promotion?" or "Why wasn't I assigned to that project?" You would coach the employee by providing information about why the person was considered for the opportunity (his or her strengths), why ultimately the opportunity was not provided to the employee this time, and what the employee can do to increase his or her chance of obtaining the opportunity next time.

Question: Won't employees perceive being selected for the high potential program as a guarantee of employment or promotion?

Answer: Employees could perceive this, so it is important to make sure they understand the program is not a guarantee of employment or promotion through the following communication methods:

❑ This can be included in a notification letter provided to the high potential employee, if you choose to use this as part of your notification process.

❑ This can be included in the "Talking Points" document that leaders will use to communicate the program to the high potential employees.

❑ Most importantly, hold "Kickoff Meetings" with the high potential employees to ensure they all hear the same positive messages about their participation in the program, as well as clear messages that they program does not provide these guarantees.

The purpose of the Kickoff Meeting is to provide an initial communication forum for the high potential employees to explain what to expect from the program, and what is expected of the high potential employee.

One More Closing Argument for Notification of High Potentials

If nothing else has yet convinced you that it is worth the risk of the potential morale issues and "high potential big head" issues that most people are concerned about, to gain the retention and focused development advantages you achieve with high potential notification, consider this one final thought – healthy competition is a driving force in the development of new and better products, services, and employee performance.

It is interesting that all throughout our lives (at least in the United States culture), we are taught to compete with others, or with a standard to achieve, in order to be successful. We continuously learn how to handle acceptance or rejection based on our performance (i.e. trying out for the football team, running for student council, qualifying for an academic award, being accepted into the college of your choice) but somehow in the workplace the idea of selecting individuals for a focused development program based on their demonstrated performance and potential becomes a threatening idea to some.

Companies must compete every day with other companies, with external market forces, and with changing conditions. Employees are competing every day to meet and exceed goals, to be rewarded through compensation, recognition, and promotional opportunities. What would happen if we decided not to promote employees anymore, because of the potential morale issue it imposes upon employees who may desire the job but are not selected?

Choose the Best Answer for Your Organization

We hope the content of this chapter provides the information you will need to discuss this question with others in your organization and to come to a conclusion everyone is comfortable with. If you decide not to notify high potential employees, the entire Talent Review and Succession Planning process is still one of the most valuable actions you can take to identify strengths and development needs to enhance your leadership benchstrength, so please go forth and continue on through this book to plan, implement, and measure your program.

> *The most important thing is to select the high potential selection, notification, and development approach that is the best match for your company's culture and readiness stage for leadership development.*

Checkpoint: Summarizing Notification Decisions

Use this section to summarize your thoughts from this chapter regarding the goals you want to implement for your high potential notification processes.

Ratings: 1 = Part of our current strategy

2 = Part of our future strategy

3 = Not Applicable or To Be Determined

1   2   3

☐ ☐ ☐   After the Talent Assessment and Talent Review processes are completed, we plan to notify all employees of their perceived talent contribution in the company.

☐ ☐ ☐   We will notify the individuals who have been identified as high potentials during our leadership talent review process.

☐ ☐ ☐   We will notify the managers of the identified high potentials, and work with them to develop these employees.

☐ ☐ ☐   We will notify our Human Resource partners of the individuals who have been selected as high potentials, and work with them to develop these employees.

☐ ☐ ☐   We will notify our critical experts to communicate the value and contribution they bring to the organization, and to increase their retention.

☐ ☐ ☐   We will provide opportunities for our critical experts to teach and mentor others in the organization in their area of expertise.

☐ ☐ ☐   We will provide special compensation or financial retention rewards to those who have been identified as critical experts.

☐ ☐ ☐   We will provide a special development program for individuals who have been identified as "high potentials" during our leadership talent review process.

Chapter Five

Planning the Talent Assessment Process

Now you've created your High Potential strategy and plans, and you are ready to launch the first phase of the process that will be used to identify successors and high potentials – talent assessment.

During this phase, leaders will use tools you create (or purchase) to review and evaluate the talent and potential future leadership ability of the individuals who report to them. These tools will include objective criteria and a quantitative method for leaders to think about the talent on their team prior to the face-to-face Talent Review meeting.

This chapter provides information to prepare you for the questions that will occur during this phase of the Talent Review and Succession planning process, and for the decisions you will need to make on the following topics:

- Do we need to include a Talent Assessment phase as part of our overall Talent Review and Succession Planning process?

- As we assess our talent, how much should we factor in an individual's past performance versus an individual's perceived future potential?

- How can we measure future potential if this is behavior that has not occurred yet?

- What criteria should we use as talent assessment components?

- What type of rating system should we use in our talent assessment process?

- Who will complete the talent assessment process – all leaders, or a sub-category of leaders? Should employees complete a self talent assessment?

- What type of tool should we create or purchase for this phase of the process?

- How is a talent assessment process different from the performance appraisal process?

Advantages of Talent Assessment Project Phase

First, you may be asking if you even need to include any type of quantitative talent assessment in your overall process. This phase adds length to your overall project timeline, and requires more time on the part of your business unit leaders to take action and to follow through with this phase. But including a Talent Assessment phase as the first step in your Talent Review and Succession Planning process presents the following advantages:

- It creates the time period and structure for leaders to spend time reviewing the talent potential of their team for the future. Often leaders are so busy tackling urgent day-to-day issues that this type of activity, while important, does not occur without a formal talent assessment process.

- It provides a quantitative, objective assessment tool to compare and contrast employees on the team against organizational-wide desired characteristics.

- It shortens the length of time needed for your face-to-face Talent Review meeting by obtaining data prior to the meeting, in the same way that on-line pre-work assigned before a training workshop can reduce the time of the workshop, while enhancing the richness of the meeting discussion.

  Starting the Talent Review meeting with a "blank sheet of paper", rather than with compiled data ready to review and discuss is like going into an individual's performance review meeting without a completed performance review to discuss.

- It helps you, as the facilitator of the Talent Review meeting, to see ahead of time how well the leaders evaluate their people and how well they understand the Talent Review process. For example, if a leader identifies an individual as both a current and future successor at the same time, or if a leader nominates 70% of their team as high potentials, you can prepare questions and coaching ahead of the meeting around these issues.

- It creates the best possible fairness and objectivity around the Talent Review process, as all employees are assessed, and therefore all employees are evaluated as successors or as high potentials before decisions are made.

Identifying Your Talent Assessment Criteria

You and your organization have several decisions to make as you are creating your talent assessment process. We recommend that you document your decisions and your procedures clearly as you progress through these questions, to establish the logic behind your decisions for any future legal reviews of your process that may occur either within your company or by external agencies that regulate internal and external recruiting processes.

First, you will need to decide as an organization the criteria for the future competencies that are most critical for successful leadership in your company. Be absolutely sure you are identifying and assessing for future competency needs; otherwise, all you will be doing is assessing and developing people for where you are today, which will not proactively enable you to prepare your organization for future success.

One question many organizations wrestle with is how much to weight successful past performance and how much to weight future potential when identifying high potentials and successors. After all, we know that past performance is the best indicator of future performance, and we use this knowledge in the form of behavioral interviewing when hiring new employees. So certainly we want to include an evaluation of past performance when identifying our future leaders.

On the other hand, we also know about the "Peter Principle", and we have all seen leaders who perform well in one situation, and then as the company changes and grows, their abilities do not change and grow to continue at the same level of success. So we know that we also need to work to assess future potential, which some would certainly argue is harder to assess, because we are trying to evaluate something that has not occurred yet!

There is no "perfect answer" or exact best practice regarding the question of how much to factor in past performance versus future potential in the talent assessment process. However, many companies work with a balanced approach – factoring in both past performance and future potential at an approximately 50/50 rate.

Some companies use the "9-box" approach (see the Definitions section of this book for more information on the 9-box tool) to balance past performance criteria and future potential. When identifying your assessment criteria, simply work to achieve a balance between past performance and future potential, as needed for your organization's business.

For example, an industry that is changing at a very rapid pace may want to place more weight on the future potential criteria items, whereas a more established industry may value past performance more. When selecting your talent assessment criteria, you will also want to balance the need to select enough criteria to create a valid and comprehensive assessment, while not "overdoing" the number of criteria, which would make the assessment process too cumbersome, time-consuming, and potentially confusing.

The table on the following page provides examples of talent assessment criteria that can be used to measure past performance and future potential. Your own talent assessment criteria can include a combination of criteria that measures these two factors.

Potential Talent Assessment Criteria Options

Past Performance Criteria	Future Potential Criteria
Performance Appraisal Rating – use each individual's most recent performance rating, or an average rating of multiple years of performance appraisals.	**Learning Agility** – Includes characteristics such as an ability to learn new tasks very quickly, work successfully in an ambiguous situation, adapt to change quickly, create innovative solutions, etc.
360 Feedback Data (not recommended for use as talent assessment data unless your organization includes 360 ratings as part of your performance appraisal process)	**Advancement Potential** – You will need to clearly define this term for your organization. For example, it could be defined as the ability to advance at least 2 levels within the next 5 years, or the ability to advance to the next level within the coming year, etc.
Behavior Dimensions (i.e. rating employees based on their behaviors as aligned with your corporate values or competencies)	**Relocation Ability** – This factor may not be applicable in your organization, or it may be critical if your organization is spread nationally or globally.
Past Advancement History – Typically, high potential employees will have a history of rapid advancement; therefore, their history of advancement could be used as an assessment factor.	**Advancement Aspiration** – Some employees are seen as having the ability to advance into higher-level positions, *but they do not desire any further advancement*. This aspiration level is an important factor to consider when identifying successors and high potentials.
Company Tenure – Your organization may want to establish guidelines regarding the length of time an employee must be employed with your company before being assessed (i.e. 90 days, 6 months), and before an employee is eligible to be nominated as a high potential employee, to ensure adequate time to observe an employee's performance and behaviors.	**Formal Assessments of Future Potential** – Your assessment process may include formal assessments of leadership ability and potential that can be purchased and/or administered by external vendors.
Industry Knowledge – Including an assessment in this category may be especially important if your industry is very complex.	**Leadership Ability** – Rate an individual's future leadership potential based on your organization's leadership competencies, and/or on effective leadership behaviors such as coaching skills, strategic thinking, interpersonal skills, etc.
Multiple Leader Recommendations – Your assessment process could include a requirement for a recommendation from at least one other leader in the organization for an employee to be nominated as a high potential or successor.	

Can We Really Predict Potential?

One criticism of the practice of identifying high potentials and successors pertains to the validity of one's ability to measure and identify future potential – how can you rate or measure behavior that has not yet occurred? Some of your internal or external clients will question whether the prediction of future leadership talent is possible. Others will want the process to result in 100% accurate predictions, every time.

But in any business, leaders actually measure behavior that has not yet occurred on a regular basis. Companies have been doing this for years, using other structured processes that are designed to identify the best decision or direction to take.

Consider these examples of other business processes that are designed to make predictions about the future:

Mergers and Acquisitions: <u>The Due Diligence Process</u>

New Product Development: <u>Market Analysis</u>

Advertising: <u>Focus Group Feedback</u>

Hiring New Employees: <u>The Interview Process</u>

Developing New Technology: <u>User Requirements Analysis</u>

Are any of these business processes "foolproof"? Will using a business process like these ensure a mistake is never made? Any business leader knows they are definitely not foolproof, but they are the best tools available that are designed to analyze data, feedback, and perceptions in order to make the best business decision possible.

The Talent Assessment process is simply another business process that is designed to analyze data, feedback, and perceptions about people in order to make the best decision possible to prepare and develop the most promising leadership talent for the future of the company. Like any other business process, it is not foolproof, but it is certainly far better than simply hoping that the best talent in the organization will emerge on it's own, and assuming these individuals will somehow receive the development they need to be prepared for a new leadership role at the right time.

When organizations make projections about the potential of an individual, their perception is based on the performance they have already observed, as well as the individual's ability to learn and perform successfully in new roles, which is why it is so important to include a rating of one's "learning agility" when considering an employee's future potential. As organizational change and the pace of information exchange in a global economy continues to expand, one's learning agility, including the ability to demonstrate flexibility and the ability to be successful in an environment of changing priorities, will be a clear key to successful leadership and work performance.

High Potentials Versus High Performers

One error that leaders often make when identifying successors and high potentials is confusing a **high performer** with a **high potential**. This is easy to confuse because a high potential should also always be a high performer, but a high performer may not be a high potential, because they may not have the desire to advance further, or they may lack relocation ability, or they may lack the strategic thinking ability that will be needed for them to have the potential to advance further.

There are multiple factors that could restrict a high performer from being a high potential. These factors often change over time, changing one's potential. For example, an employee may not be able or willing to relocate until a factor of their personal situation changes, and then they may have complete flexibility to relocate. This is one reason it is important to conduct talent assessments and talent review meetings on a regular and ongoing basis.

> *Help your leaders understand the difference – not all high performers are high potentials.*

Leaders are also sometimes confused on the difference between the talent assessment process and the performance appraisal process. This is important for you, as the leader of one or both of these processes, to understand and to be able to articulate.

The table on the following page outlines the similarities and differences between these two processes.

Performance Appraisal Process Versus Talent Assessment Process

Similarities	Differences
The factors rated in both processes may overlap – for example, you may decide to rate leadership behaviors in both your appraisal process and your talent assessment process. However, you might use different rating systems and/or different definitions, in order to capture future leadership competency needs.	The performance appraisal process only measures past performance, but the talent assessment process is designed to also rate and predict future potential, especially future leadership potential.
To be most effective, all employees should be rated in both the performance appraisal and talent assessment processes. The process should be consistent company-wide for all employees.	The performance appraisal process is designed to provide both written and verbal feedback to employees regarding their on-the-job performance, whereas talent assessment does not include a feedback process. In fact, your talent assessment ratings may be a completely confidential process that is never discussed with the employee, to increase validity of the ratings; leaders may provide more honest ratings when they know they don't have to discuss them with employees. The talent assessment ratings simply provide a method for leaders to review their talent as objectively as possible.
Depending on the structure of your processes, there may be other similarities. For example, you may use an online rating system for both processes, you may conduct both processes within the same time period of the year, etc.	The goals of the two processes are different: - The performance appraisal measures job performance the employee has demonstrated in the past year, based on written goals provided to the employee - The talent assessment measures past performance and future potential in order to identify successors, leadership needs, and/or high potentials

Timing of the Talent Assessment Process

When determining when the talent assessment process should take place, there are multiple factors to consider:

- Will the entire organization complete the assessment process within the same time period of the year, or should we identify assessment time periods for business groups factoring in their business needs and "peak seasons" to help ensure they will have time to focus on the process?

- Should we incorporate the talent assessment process as part of the performance appraisal process, or at least have both processes take place at the same time?

- What company-wide business activities should be considered when identifying a time period? For example, scheduling talent assessment during the budget process or during the company's annual financial report period would very likely decrease compliance with the talent assessment process, and/or the time leaders are willing to spend on the process.

The answer to the first question – whether to conduct talent assessment at one time in the company or spread the process out over the year based on business group needs – will depend on the size of your organization, and the size of the group assigned to lead the talent assessment and talent review process.

For example, it may simply not be practical to conduct talent assessment all at one time throughout the company. On the other hand, if the size of your organization leading the talent assessment and talent review process is one person, it may not be practical to spread this activity out over the entire year.

Regarding the second question – whether to conduct performance appraisals and talent assessments at the same time – please know that this is not a recommended process. Combining these two processes further creates confusion between the differences between them, and leaders may decrease the time they spend on the talent assessment process, because they are already overwhelmed with trying to complete performance appraisals on time.

One advantage of scheduling both processes at the same time is that leaders are already in the mode of "thinking about their people", and if your performance appraisal process includes career and development plan discussions, the leaders should then have current information from the employee regarding their advancement aspirations, their relocation ability, etc.

As another option, talent assessment activities could immediately follow the performance appraisal process, with the "communication spin" that leaders have just completed the measurement of past performance through the appraisal process, and they are now being asked to predict future potential through the talent assessment process.

And of course there is no "perfect time" to complete the talent assessment process. At any one time, there are always many priorities going on in the company that you will be competing with. Choose your best timing strategy, obtain the executive sponsorship and support you will need, and remember to be both flexible and persistent to drive momentum for the strategy.

Talent Assessment Rating Systems

Whether your talent assessment process is completed through computer spreadsheets or through an online web-based system, the rating process you use is critical. Remember to spend extensive time writing and calibrating the definitions of each assessment factor and of each rating carefully – once your talent assessment is launched to the organization, you will not be able to change these without risking an inconsistent and invalid assessment process.

Another factor to consider is what rating options you will want to provide to leaders. The important thing is to "remove the gray" from the assessment process to clearly identify high potential employees in the organization, and to distinguish between the "high performers" and the "high potentials", as discussed earlier in this chapter. Some examples to consider:

- If you use an "even" rating scale, such as 1, 2, 3, 4, leaders will not have an option to rate someone as "average". Instead they will have to make a choice between employees who are below standard, below average, above average, or exceptional.

- If you use the exact same rating scale as your performance appraisal process, leaders will most likely copy the same ratings they used for that process. This may not be desirable, because the goals of the appraisal process and the talent assessment process are different.

- If you use a rating scale of 1, 2, 3, 4, and 5, it may be hard to differentiate the highest performers, as leaders will tend to overuse the 4 and the 5 ratings. Check the bell curve of your performance appraisal process to see if leaders in your organization have a tendency to over-inflate ratings.

- Another rating system to consider is a "skip rating" system – forcing the use of ratings 1, 3, and 5, as an example. This forces the leaders to identify employees performing at a "below average" rating, those who are performing up to standard, and employees who are exceptional.

  Create very clear distinctions between the definitions of these ratings, and build your system to reject any attempts to enter ratings of 2 or 4, which would "soften" the results. Your goal is to draw out the top talent of the organization, and to truly differentiate the exceptional, high potential individuals.

- Some organizations may consider using a forced ranking system within their talent assessment process, if this already fits their culture and needs. In this system, leaders would be forced to identify specific percentages of their organizations within each of the ratings, eliminating the "over-inflation" of ratings.

Talent Assessment Participants

Another question to answer before launching your talent assessment process is who should complete a talent assessment. The answer to this question depends largely on your Talent Review and Succession Planning goals, which you identified earlier in this book. For example, if you want to contain your process to focus on the senior leadership level only, you will only have the executive leadership level complete the talent assessment process.

If your talent assessment process will include nomination of high potentials, this will be a factor in your decision regarding who completes the talent assessment process. For example, if you have multiple categories of high potentials (i.e. individual contributor high potentials, manager high potentials, executive high potentials, etc.), and if all employees in the company are eligible for the high potential program, it will be important to include all leaders in the talent assessment process.

To further increase the richness of the talent assessment data, to increase the fairness of the process, and to obtain information that leaders may not be aware of, you can also choose to ask employees to complete a talent assessment on themselves. Employees can enter this data as a first stage of the talent assessment data. Leaders can then view this data prior to completing their talent assessment on each member of the team.

Employees can provide information such as current relocation ability, career interests, and ability to self-evaluate accurately, etc. It also involves the employees in the process. However, this removes the option of keeping the talent assessment confidential, which may reduce the candor leaders use to enter ratings and other data points.

Another option is to ask employees to provide or enter this type of data on a system for use during the Talent Review meeting at a later point, but not to ask employees to participate in their own talent assessment. Regardless, it is critical that the leaders are aware of each employee's leadership advancement desire, relocation ability, career interests, appetite for feedback and development, etc. in order to make the best selections for successors and high potential employees.

Remember, it is critical to retain the confidentiality of the leader's ratings, no matter which process is used. Again, the talent assessment process is not a feedback system, and confidentiality increases honesty in the talent assessment ratings.

Choosing Your Tools

Depending upon the size of your organization, and the size of your budget, you can use a computer spreadsheet form for your talent assessment process. Create a form with automated calculations based on the ratings entered by leaders. Many companies use this type of talent assessment process – even large organizations with sophisticated talent assessment strategies.

However...

WARNING

WARNING

WARNING

A computer spreadsheet process will result in an extensive amount of manual work. This will include hours to receive and sort the completed Excel talent assessments from each leader, compile the results, track completion progress manually, continuously update the spreadsheet, etc.

If you are thinking that you will be using a computer spreadsheet talent assessment process, most likely you are making that decision due to concerns regarding the cost of an external talent management system. As an alternate option, check with your IT department to determine if they could create an online web-based system internally. This will most likely be your lowest cost option, if you keep the format and process simple.

However, you can also check with external vendors who specialize in creating survey and assessment systems of all types – you may find the cost of purchasing this type of system to be well worth the time you will save in reducing manual work. In addition, a user-friendly, web-based system will be well received by leaders, saving them time, and increasing the credibility of the process.

If your Talent Management system can be tied to your overall HR system, to automatically populate data such as employee names, titles, performance review ratings, etc., this will also decrease your work time, increase the accuracy of the process, and make the system more user-friendly for leaders.

> *A piece of advice: Make sure your talent assessment process is well defined, tested, and agreed upon internally before investing too much in your talent assessment system.*

When creating your talent assessment tool(s), remember to build in the confidentiality aspect of the system, using security methods such as user identification codes and passwords. It is important for leaders to feel confident that the system is secure and that their ratings will not be viewed by employees.

Components of Your Talent Assessment System

You will also need to determine what data to capture from leaders and employees prior to the Talent Review meeting. For example, is it better to ask leaders to create draft succession plans prior to the Talent Review meeting, or just start with a blank succession plan and fill it in during the Talent Review meeting discussion? (Our opinion is that it is better to ask them prior to the meeting so you have a base to start the discussion from, but that may not be practical for the size and culture of your organization.)

In general, the more data you can capture, review, and compile before the face-to-face Talent Review meeting, the better, because you will be more prepared for the Talent Review meeting and the length of time the Talent Review meeting will take is reduced, which will make your leaders happy.

However, this must be balanced with the time it will take the leaders to complete the talent assessment process. If you try to "stuff" too much into the talent assessment tool the leaders will be less likely to complete the process and you will receive more questions from leaders who may become frustrated or confused about what is expected from them.

You will also need to decide if your talent assessment process will include only a ratings system to evaluate talent and future potential, or if you want to include additional actions in the tool, such as:

- A 9-Box Exercise (see the Definitions section at the beginning of this book)

- Nomination of High Potentials

- Nomination of Technical Experts / Critical Personnel

- Succession Plan Entries / Updates

- Build or Update Online Employee Profiles / Competencies

- Space for open-ended comments from leaders

Think of the talent assessment process as a time to "turn over some rocks". Leaders may find that Joe Ellison has been sitting across from them for a year but they didn't realize he has five years of experience leading a highly successful sales team, and that he would be perfect for a future planned position or project that will require this skill.

Build your system to match the leadership needs and culture of your company. Your final assessment process should align with the goals you identified earlier in this book. If you have any "hot buttons" in your company pertaining to behaviors that are critical to your company's success and mission, such as exceptional customer service, flawless integrity, etc., be sure to include these behaviors in your assessment process.

This is also the right time to determine what factors you plan to discuss in your face-to-face Talent Review meetings, because you may want to include entries in your talent assessment system to gather some data "up front" for discussion in the meeting.

For example, if you plan to discuss the "Position Vacancy Risk" of each leader during the Talent Review meeting, you could add an entry into your talent assessment system for leaders to rate each employee on this factor, which enables you to bring prepared and compiled data to the Talent Review meeting.

But again, be careful not to add too many components to the talent assessment system, to avoid making it too cumbersome for leaders to complete. Just as establishing 23 leadership competencies in your company would be too overwhelming to be successful, including too many talent assessment components tends to "water down" the process. Focus on what is most important for your company. Best practice research suggests that including approximately 5-10 talent assessment components in your tool is practical and comprehensive enough to provide adequate leadership behavior data points.

Avoid including too much "commentary" or open-ended data in your talent assessment system, which will be difficult to wade through and analyze. However, having one or two commentary sections may add important data to the process. For example, what qualifications and competencies do your successors need to become more prepared for the incumbent leader's position?

Final Ideas for Talent Assessment

A well-designed talent assessment system will greatly increase the value of the face-to-face Talent Review meeting, increase the validity and credibility of the entire process, and will increase your ability to be fully prepared for the Talent Review meetings. Some final pieces of advice when building or purchasing your talent assessment tool:

- Build in some type of print capability for leaders to print a final talent assessment chart of their team, or a 9-box chart of their team, or their succession plan – whatever makes sense for the system you create. This enables leaders to keep a record of their entries, and provides a document for them to use when discussing their talent assessment entries with their own leaders.

- The talent assessment tool should not be a "stand-alone" activity – the assessment process should include discussions between leaders and employees to share information about career and development interests. Leaders should also discuss the succession plans, talent assessment results and high potential nominations they have entered into the talent assessment tool with their leaders.

- If your talent assessment process will include additional actions such as nominating high potentials and creating initial succession plans, build the system to ensure the talent assessment process takes place first, so leaders can view their compiled talent assessment data for their team before making the nomination decisions.

- Whether your internal IT department is creating your talent management system or you are working with an external vendor to build a customized system for your company, be sure to build at least two phases of system testing into your project plan. Include testers from your company who are located in various building sites and locations.

- As much as you will want your talent assessment process to be "paper free", it is a good idea to create a back-up paper based talent assessment form. This can be used for any leader who simply will not complete the form online, by leaders who:

  o Travel extensively (they can complete the paper form on a plane)

- o Are having technical troubles when they use your online talent assessment system

- o May not have access to a computer system.

    If you are lucky, you won't need to use this paper-based form, but chances are good that you will need it, so it is best to create it proactively. If you provide this option, you will also need a plan for how the data that has been written on the paper form will be transferred to the system (keeping in mind the high level of confidentiality required for talent assessment ratings).

- If you build an online talent assessment system, create a method that will group the data into the same categories as your Talent Review meetings, to ensure you can create reports that are grouped by location, business unit, etc. as needed.

    For example, if you will be holding your Talent Review meetings based on location, ask the leader to enter their location as they log onto the talent assessment system. If you will be holding your Talent Review meetings by functional group, ask the leader to enter (or select from a drop down list) their functional group as they log onto the system. This will save you time by grouping your data into the report categories you will need as you prepare for the face-to-face Talent Review meeting.

Finally, don't lose sight of the fact that you are evaluating people and leadership needs for the future. Future potential must be measured against your future leadership competency needs, or you will simply be continuing the status quo. Creating a well-designed talent assessment system will "set the stage" for a successful Talent Review and Succession Planning initiative, and creates the framework for the Talent Review meeting discussions. Be sure to build plenty of time into your project plan to create a thorough and user-friendly talent assessment tool.

Checkpoint: Talent Assessment Goals

Use this section to summarize your thoughts from this chapter regarding the goals you want to implement for your talent assessment process.

Ratings: 1 = Part of our current strategy

2 = Part of our future strategy

3 = Not Applicable or To Be Determined

1   2   3

☐ ☐ ☐   We will implement a Talent Assessment process that leaders can use to objectively rate each of their direct reports regarding their future potential in the organization.

☐ ☐ ☐   Our Talent Assessment process will include an option for leaders to nominate individuals for the high potential program.

☐ ☐ ☐   We will create (or work with an external vendor to create, purchase, and/or customize) an online Talent Management system the data entry and storage of succession plans, talent assessment data, employee profiles, high potential information.

☐ ☐ ☐   We will provide a 9-box tool that will enable leaders to create and/or view a cross-section of their employees based on their past performance and future potential.

☐ ☐ ☐   Our Talent Assessment process will take place at this time of the year:

_____

☐ ☐ ☐   The following leaders will complete a Talent Assessment of their employees: _____

Chapter Six

The Talent Review Meeting: What is It?

The Talent Review meeting (which goes by various names in the organizations who are already using this type of process) is a structured and facilitated session designed for the discussion of current and future leadership talent in the organization. Typically, the Talent Review meeting is preceded by the Talent Assessment process, and compiled or summarized data is reviewed and/or provided in the meeting, as a starting point for the meeting discussions.

If the Talent Assessment process is the quantitative step of the Talent Management and High Potential identification process, then the Talent Review meeting is the qualitative stage of this process. Between these two phases of the process, the results can change significantly, based on discussions and consensus of the Talent Review meeting participants. In addition, the validity of the data is increased, as multiple data points are used in the decision-making process.

A Talent Review meeting may be a facilitated session with one business leader, or with multiple leaders all attending together, depending on the situation and the need. Primarily, the remainder of this book will focus on Talent Review meetings that are attended by multiple business leaders, participating in the meeting together.

Talent Review Meeting Objectives

The primary objective of the Talent Review meeting is for leaders to discuss the available and emerging talent in the organization (some organizations also discuss potential external talent in these sessions) that is needed to achieve the business goals.

For example, if a critical business goal of the company is to implement a new quality strategy and process throughout the company, then it will be important to identify talent that can lead, design, and implement this initiative.

The Talent Review meeting will also increase the visibility of the talent in the business units and within the organization. If cross-functional Talent Review sessions are held, the visibility of talent that can move to another business unit or to another location or country is enhanced.

The Talent Review meeting provides the time for leaders to stop and think about their people. Rightly so, business leaders focus most of their time on the business on a daily basis, addressing urgent situations and planning their next business strategies. Implementing a Talent Review process places the business planning actions of talent identification and people development at the same level as other important business responsibilities.

81

In addition, the Talent Review meeting provides an objective facilitator and a structured process for leaders to follow, which provides consistency and more of the "science" to the talent discussions. Senior leaders can observe the skill and abilities of their mid-level managers to accurately assess and discuss talent.

And finally, when the Talent Review meeting is attended by multiple business leaders together, it provides opportunities for managers to hear multiple perspectives about the employees who report to them, both positive perceptions and constructive feedback. It provides a time for them to learn "the buzz" about their own employees. This information can be used in an appropriate way to provide feedback to the employee to help him or her leverage strengths and develop in areas of perceived weakness.

Identifying Your Talent Review Meeting Discussion Topics

There are many different agenda items you may want to include in your Talent Review meeting – select the discussion items that meet your organization's needs:

❑ **The group's business goals – this may include short term goals, long term goals, and the future vision of the group or organization**

As discussed earlier in this chapter, your primary objective is to ensure you have talent ready and prepared to lead and achieve your business goals. Therefore, it is an excellent idea to ask the most senior leader attending the meeting to be prepared to begin the meeting by discussing the current and future business goals, as well as the talent being prepared to lead the goals, and potential talent gaps that need to be filled to achieve the goals.

❑ **The leadership competencies the business group will need to demonstrate to achieve their goals**

This discussion may include the overall leadership competencies expected in the organization, or it may also include specific and additional competencies the business unit will need to achieve their goals. For example, the company may have a leadership competency need in the area of strategic planning. In addition to this, the Sales group may have a more specific competency need in the area of strategically identifying new customer markets.

❑ **The current open leadership positions in the group, and the future leadership needs**

This might include a discussion of critical positions in the group, developmental positions to be created, future positions planned for the coming year, etc. This may include retirement plans that have been formally expressed and documented, and the succession plan that will require specific focus in the coming months or years to ensure the gap the retiring leader leaves will be filled.

❑ **Overall leadership population statistics (see the Metrics chapter of this book for ideas on potential statistics to include)**

Often, the meeting will include a review of the statistics of the overall leadership population, to provide a high level overview at the beginning of the meeting. For example, the Talent Review meeting participants may want to review the ratio of the leadership population to the employee population, the diversity statistics of the population, the percentages of leaders within each management level in the organization, etc.

❑ **A review of any important definitions – such as your organization's definition of a high potential, of a successor, etc.**

Even though you have included these definitions on your talent assessment and communication tools, it is a <u>very</u> good idea to review them again at the beginning of your Talent Review meeting, to make sure everyone is "on the same page" and to allow time for questions and clarity. You may even need to refer to them or read them again at a future point in the meeting, if you find that the leaders are forgetting the definitions or straying from them significantly.

❑ **A career discussion pertaining to leaders in the business group**

This may include current company tenure, date of last lateral or promotional move for each individual, risk of the individual leaving the organization (vacancy risk), the impact of this risk, relocation ability, career readiness for another position, and potential positions or other business units each individual could move into.

❑ **An overview of the profile or resume of each leader, to increase the visibility of talents and skills throughout the business group (be sure to identify what "level" of leaders will be discussed prior to the meeting)**

The Talent Review facilitator may want to provide a copy of the resume of each individual to be discussed in the meeting, or a book of leader profiles for each meeting participant. Ideally, if you have a Talent Management system, you could project an image of each individual's profile on the wall during the meeting, and avoid having to prepare copies or books for everyone.

❑ **The strengths and development needs of each leader**

A discussion of the strengths and development needs of each individual discussed in the meeting is a "staple" of most Talent Review sessions. Our normal practice is to provide the first opportunity to discuss these strengths and development needs to the individual's direct manager, and then ask others who have worked with the individual to provide their additional perspectives. It is important to clearly and accurately document these discussions.

❑ **Leadership ability, including a discussion of behaviors pertaining to coaching and developing people, thinking strategically, hiring talent, etc.**

Most Talent Review meetings are designed to review future leadership talent; therefore, it is important to discuss specific leadership behaviors that have been observed for each individual, such as their ability to identify talent, coach employees, motivate others, etc. Sometimes these perceptions are discussed during the strengths and development needs discussion, but including a specific topic on Leadership Ability ensures this area is thoroughly covered during the meeting.

❑ **Development action plans for each leader, or for specific individuals such as successors and/or high potentials**

After discussing the strengths, next potential career path, development needs, leadership ability, etc. of each individual, discuss the action plans for the coming year that will address the points made during the discussion.

Action plans will include a wide variety of activities, such as a new job assignment, an HR action to be addressed (such as a compensation review or performance improvement plan to be drafted), a mentor to be assigned to the individual, a workshop to attend, or a project that will serve to develop the competencies of the individual.

Discussing action plans during the meeting serves multiple purposes. First, there is the advantage of having multiple people in the room who can generate effective development actions, including organizational development and human resource professionals who have knowledge of and access to a wide variety of learning resources.

Secondly, discussing these actions plans and documenting them during the meeting increases the "buy-in" and accountability of the leaders, increasing the follow-through and support of the leaders as they develop their employees in the coming months.

❑ **A review of the nominated high potentials to discuss and agree on final participants for the high potential program**

Depending on the size and the need of the organization or business unit, the Talent Review facilitator may elect to include a discussion and consensus action to finalize the nominated list of high potential leaders. Or, this discussion may take place during a separate meeting or in a separate process.

The advantage of discussing and confirming the high potential population in the Talent Review meeting is that it is often a natural discussion flow to review the strengths, development needs, and leadership ability of each leader, and to move into a discussion of their future potential in the organization. In addition, it is important that the business unit leaders all agree on the high potentials within their work team.

❑ **A discussion of the current and/or open expatriate positions in the group, and/or individuals in the group who are currently on an expatriate job assignment**

Global organizations will typically include a discussion of job assignments that are currently in progress in other countries, job assignments that could be initiated for development, and individuals who are nearing the completion of their job assignment and will be ready to return to a new role in the near future.

❑ **A review of the succession plans for the group**

We recommend that the group reviews a compiled plan of the successor nominations for the entire business unit or work group, to identify individuals who might be successors for more than one position, to discuss potential successors from other business groups, and to review development actions for successors, especially successors who are not currently ready for the incumbent's position.

While some organizations may have concerns about leaders viewing each other's succession plans at the peer level, this type of cross-functional discussion will generate new ideas for potential successors, as well as different perspectives on the "readiness" of each successor, and the action plans that are needed to develop each successor.

To date, we have not observed any issues that have ever occurred as a result of peers viewing and discussing each other's succession plans, but we have observed a great benefit that occurs through increasing the validity and agreement of the succession plans, and the visibility of the talent in the group.

Like the discussion of high potentials, some organizations conduct succession plan discussions in a separate meeting from the overall Talent Review meeting, to focus more attention on this important activity, and to "break up" the extensive amount of time needed for multiple Talent Review discussion topics.

❑ **A review of most critical positions in the business group or organization**

In addition to discussing people, the Talent Review meeting can include a discussion of the most critical positions to focus on for recruiting and development efforts. This is not to say that the "other jobs" are not important. But, the reality is that it is probably more important, as an example, to have a highly effective leader for the client that provides the most revenue for the company.

This identification of critical positions is not an assessment of the person who is currently in the role, but it is an evaluation of the position itself. By identifying the most critical roles in the organization, the human resources team, recruiters, and the business unit leaders can focus more of their time on these positions.

Remember: Bite Off What You Can Chew

In this chapter, we have provided an extensive list of potential topics to include on your Talent Review meeting agenda. This is not an indication that you need to include ALL of them. We have tried to provide a very comprehensive list (although many organizations may have other Talent Review agenda topics) for you to select the ones that will work most effectively in your organization.

In addition, if this is your first year to implement a Talent Review meeting process, consider selecting only the most appropriate (and foundational) topics to implement this year, with the thought in mind that you can continue to add additional agenda items in future years.

Checkpoint: Talent Review Meeting Topics

Use this section to summarize your thoughts from this chapter regarding the discussion topics you plan to include in your Talent Review meeting.

Ratings: **1 = Part of our current strategy**

2 = Part of our future strategy

3 = Not Applicable or To Be Determined

1   2   3

☐ ☐ ☐   We will discuss the organization's business goals, and the leadership competencies and talent that will be needed to achieve the goals

☐ ☐ ☐   We will discuss the current open leadership positions in the group, and the future anticipated leadership positions that may become vacant or may be created in the coming year

☐ ☐ ☐   We will review the overall leadership and employee population statistics for the business unit, such as the number of employees, the ratio of leaders to employees, the diversity of the group, etc.

☐ ☐ ☐   We will include a review of the definitions of high potentials and successors in the Talent Review meeting

☐ ☐ ☐   We will review each leader's career history, future career interests, their readiness to move to a new position, and future potential career moves

☐ ☐ ☐   We will review a profile or resume of each leader to increase our understanding of the work experience, skills, education, etc. of each leader

☐ ☐ ☐   We will discuss the strengths of each leader

☐ ☐ ☐   We will discuss the development needs of each leader

☐ ☐ ☐   We will identify career and development action plans for each leader

☐ ☐ ☐   We will discuss the leadership ability and future leadership potential of each leader

☐ ☐ ☐   We will discuss and confirm nominated high potentials in the Talent Review meeting

Checkpoint: Talent Review Meeting Topics (Continued)

Use this section to summarize your thoughts from this chapter regarding the discussion topics you plan to include in your Talent Review meeting.

Ratings: 1 = Part of our current strategy

2 = Part of our future strategy

3 = Not Applicable or To Be Determined

1   2   3

☐ ☐ ☐   We will complete a "Nine-Box exercise" for leaders in each business function, to assess both their current performance and their future potential in the organization. (See *Terms and Definitions* in this book for a definition of the Nine-Box chart.)

☐ ☐ ☐   We will discuss the vacancy risk of each leader, and the impact if they left the organization

☐ ☐ ☐   We will identify leaders who are ready for a career move (either a lateral or promotional move), and proactively work with them to identify a more challenging position for them in the organization.

☐ ☐ ☐   We will identify the most critical positions in the organization

☐ ☐ ☐   We will discuss current, open, and returning expatriate job assignments

☐ ☐ ☐   We will include a discussion of the succession plans for the group in the Talent Review meeting

☐ ☐ ☐   As a part of our Talent Review process, we will identify leaders who are not performing up to the goals and expectations for their position, and determine an action plan that will best address the situation

☐ ☐ ☐   We will identify leaders who are perceived to be "blockers" to high potential employees in the business group. (See *Terms and Definitions* in this book for a definition a "blocker".)

☐ ☐ ☐   We will include these additional topics in our Talent Review meeting:

_____

_____

Chapter Seven

Collaboration with Internal Partners

To launch a successful Talent Review and Succession Planning process, you will need the cooperation and assistance from your human resource partners (and other internal partners) within the organization. These partners could include other training and organizational development personnel, regional human resources personnel, or even global human resource partners.

You may need the assistance of these human resource partners to implement the process within their business unit or region. You will also need their help to communicate the strategy and plans in these same areas, to answer questions that employees and leaders may have, and to help bring participants "to the table", so to speak.

You can think of your role as the one who plans and cooks the food for the Talent Management buffet table (or to find someone else to cater it), but you need your human resource partners to tell others how great the food will be, to answer questions about what will be on the menu, and most importantly, to make sure people attend the event to eat the food!

In this chapter, we will discuss what your human resource partners will need to know to be effective and willing partners in your Talent Review and Succession Planning initiative. They will have questions about your program such as:

❑ What are goals and objectives of the program, and how does it align with the corporate objectives?

❑ How will the program impact their business unit or region, both in the short term and the long term?

❑ What role will they have in this initiative? What will be expected of them?

❑ How much time will the program take on their part, and what times during the year will their role have the most significant impact on their workload?

❑ What can they expect to gain from this program? What can their business unit or region expect to gain from this program?

❑ What questions might they be asked from the employees and leaders they support, and what are the answers to these questions?

❑ What are the potential risks or issues that could occur with this program, and how can these be mitigated?

❑ What is the timeline of the program implementation?

To answer these questions, you will want to create communication and reference guide tools to provide to your human resource partners.

Communication and Reference Tools

There are several types of tools and methods you can use to achieve the collaboration and understanding of the program that you will need from your human resource partners. Below are some examples of these tools. Be sure to use multiple methods – it is unlikely that only one of them will work; you need to provide the messages multiple times and in multiple ways to reach a high level of understanding of the process throughout the company.

Simulated Talent Review Meeting

If you are implementing a Talent Review and Succession Planning program for the first time in your company, one of your biggest challenges in gaining the cooperation and assistance of your human resource partners is helping them to understand what the process is and how it works. One way to overcome this is to set up a simulated Talent Review meeting, and invite your partners to attend.

Each of your human resource partners attend the meeting and act in the role of a business unit leader – you will need to provide each of them with mock employees, giving each of them a written synopsis of their employees, including the employees' strengths, development areas, career history, leadership ability, next potential career move, etc.

Next, distribute your Talent Review meeting agenda and move through the meeting as you would for an actual Talent Review meeting. This provides an opportunity for your human resource partners to experience a meeting in a mock setting, where they can ask questions, rather than participating in this type of meeting for the first time with senior business unit leaders.

Communicate Roles Clearly

It is very important to clearly define and discuss the role each of your human resource partners will play in your Talent Review and Succession Planning process. Here are some potential actions they may have as part of their role:

- Taking your corporate communications tools – guides, reference materials, presentation slides, etc. – and "rolling out" this communication throughout the business units they support; this may include a variety of geographic regions or functional areas

- Tracking and following up with business unit leaders to complete any pre-assessment talent data they are responsible for providing (such as completing draft succession plans or nominating high potential individuals), prior to the Talent Review meeting

- Serving either as a business unit partner, or a note-taker/facilitator in the Talent Review meeting; you will need to determine if you need their participation more as an active meeting participant who provides their own data and perspectives of the leaders being discussed, or if you need their help more as an objective meeting facilitator and as an additional person to take notes during the meeting

- Identifying any special accommodations or needs the business unit will have; for example, a Talent Review meeting for a small business unit will of course be shorter in length than a larger business unit

- Working with the business unit leaders and their assistants to coordinate the important logistics of the Talent Review meeting, such as:

  o Working with the senior leader of the group to determine who should attend the Talent Review meeting; this may be the senior leader and all of his or her direct reports, but if the position levels of the direct reports varies greatly, or if there are too many direct reports, discussion may be needed to identify the most appropriate attendees

  o Finding a date for the meeting that will work for the schedules of all attendees (not an easy task)

  o Reserving a facility for the meeting (it must be a secure location due to the confidentiality of the conversations that will take place, and it should be a comfortable facility to accommodate a lengthy meeting)

  o Reserving any food or refreshments that may be needed if the meeting will take place over the lunch period

It will also be important to discuss and clarify with your human resource partners the role that you will play throughout the process. The responsibilities of your role may include:

  o Defining the philosophies and strategy you will use to define your Talent Review and Succession Planning process

  o Creating the corporate Talent Management tools and process

  o Creating the communication tools, materials, and/or presentation slides

  o Developing and updating the overall project plan for the initiative

  o Communicating progress and any changes that occur to senior leader sponsors and partners

  o Defining the Talent Review agenda and ground rules – developing and preparing all documents needed for the Talent Review meeting, to ensure corporate-wide consistency o   Identifying and clarifying the roles of all participants – typically your role will be to facilitate the meeting, or else you will need to identify a facilitator

    o   Documenting all notes and action items as discussed in the meeting

    o   Defining and creating any materials needed for the high potential notification process (if applicable in your organization)

    o   Leading the effort of follow up actions – tracking and measuring results

Presentations

Another communication method is to provide face-to-face or virtual presentations to your human resource partners, providing information and answers to all of the questions listed on page 1 of this chapter within the presentation slides.

Leader's Guide

Another tool you can create is a <u>Leader's Guide</u> that can be available online and/or distributed as a hardcopy document to all business unit leaders and partners who will be participating in the process. This document should include information about the program goals, a high level overview of the process, what the leader's role is in the process, how they can prepare for the Talent Review meeting, and what they can expect throughout the process. This information is helpful for business unit leaders, but also provides a reference guide for your internal human resource partners.

Facilitator's Guide

If any of your human resource or organizational development partners will be facilitating or co-facilitating any of your Talent Review meetings, you will want to create a <u>Facilitator's Guide</u>, which contains information and tools that pertain only to those who will be leading these meetings. The content of this guide may include:

- The role of the facilitator in the Talent Review meeting

- Materials and documents to prepare and bring to the Talent Review meeting

- Facilitator Tips and Techniques (see Chapter Seven of this book)

- The meeting agenda

- The ground rules for the meeting

- Preparing for the Talent Review meeting

Provide Updates in Human Resource Staff Meetings

Attend the staff meetings of your Human Resource partners on a regular basis throughout the Talent Review and Succession Planning process, to provide status updates and progress reports, to answer questions, and to obtain feedback from both the human resource partners and the feedback they are hearing from their business unit leaders.

Focus Group Sessions

Either as your Talent Review and Succession Planning process is moving along, or when you reach a milestone point (such as the point where all Talent Review meetings are complete), a way to encourage two-way communication and feedback about the process – what went well and what improvements are suggested – is to hold face-to-face or virtual focus group sessions with your human resource partners. Start with a list of prepared questions to obtain feedback, but also be open to a flexible agenda as long as the discussion is on target and valuable. Prepared questions may include:

- What was your own comfort level and understanding of our Talent Review and Succession Planning process before it was launched in your business unit? What is your level of comfort and understanding like at this point? How can we increase this level earlier in the process for you?

- After we communicated the process to your business unit leaders, what was their comfort level and understanding, and what is the level now? How can we increase this level earlier in the process for them?

- What is the most valuable aspect of this process, and why? What indicators cause you to believe this is the most valuable aspect of the process? What business improvements are you seeing as a result of this process?

- What was the most confusing part of the process, and why? How can we improve in this aspect as we move forward?

- What are your thoughts on the timing of the Talent Review meeting – was it too long, too short, or just right. What are your suggestions for improvements to the timing of the meeting?

- Do you feel your business unit leaders were prepared for the Talent Review and Succession Planning meeting – why or why not? What worked well to prepare them, and how can we improve in this area?

- On a scale of 1-10, with 10 being the best rating, how would you rate your business unit's level of participation and engagement in this process – explain your response.

- Regarding the communications, tools, and materials provided to you during the process, how would you describe their value, ease of use, and quantity? Were the communication tools helpful? Were there too few or too many? Did the communication materials provide enough detail about the process without being overwhelming? Why or why not?

- Did you feel you understood your role throughout the Talent Review and Succession Planning process? What worked well in clarifying your understanding of your role, and how can this be improved?

- Regarding the notification of high potential employees – what worked well and what improvements can be made to this communication process?

- What positive comments have you heard from leaders and employees in your business units regarding the Talent Review and Succession Planning process? What complaints have you heard?

- Now we are at the "follow-through" point of taking action on the notes and recommendations throughout the year, how can we support each other, and support the business units to complete these actions?

- Think about our Talent Review and Succession Planning process at an "overall" level – what additional comments do you have to either reinforce what is working well, or to improve what is not working well?

Human Resource Web Site

If your company has a resource web site that is provided just for the use of your human resource personnel, make sure you create a page on this site to post updates, documents, reference materials, and answers to frequently asked questions.

Provide "Sneak Previews" to your Human Resource Partners

Be sure to provide your human resource partners with the first look at the documents, systems, tools, and communication that will be going out to business unit leaders – they could receive calls and questions about these items from their business unit leaders as soon as they are distributed, and you definitely don't want them to feel that they are not aware of what is going on.

It is also helpful to obtain feedback from your human resource partners on the tools and materials you create for your program prior to implementation. They will be able to review these materials from the business and internal customer point of view, and they can provide a different perspective to help shape your program tools.

Don't Forget to Thank Them!

Your internal partners are absolutely critical to the success of your Talent Review and Succession Planning initiative – they will help your strategy and plans become reality throughout the company. They are your connection to the business units – your customers. They will be providing assistance, ideas, and feedback throughout the year, and they will be able to provide metrics information and the results that can be observed on-the-job within the business units they support. They will help the business unit leaders implement development actions that are identified during the Talent Review meeting.

Remember to thank them for all of the work and support they will be providing throughout the year, and always remember to continue two-way open communication with them to maintain a strong partnership with these important people.

Chapter Eight

Preparing for the Executive Presentation

You've determined the readiness level of your organization for your Talent Review and Succession Planning program, you've identified the goals for your program, and you've made key decisions about your processes and program philosophy. Now you may be asked (or you may need to ask) to present the program plans to your organization's executives to ensure agreement and understanding of your talent management strategy. This chapter will help you put together your presentation, including some sample presentation slides to help you get started.

To prepare, you will want to review the "tough questions and answers" provided in this book regarding your high potential strategic decisions. You probably will not need to cover these issues in your presentation, but you should have answers to them in your "back pocket" to be prepared. Also be prepared to be able to explain the difference between a Talent Management and Performance Review process.

You will want to summarize your goals into a concise format in your presentation. You may also want to skip ahead in this book to review and identify the metrics you plan to use from the <u>Metrics Checklist</u>.

What will your executive team be interested in? Here are some potential items of interest, but to a great extent these items will vary depending on the culture and current situation of your company:

- What is a Talent Review and Succession Planning program?

- What are the expected business results of this program?

- What is our current leadership benchstrength and what is the risk of not implementing this program?

- How does this program compare to what our competitors are doing? How does it compare to what organizations of similar size or industry are doing?

- How much will it cost?

- What is the high-level timeline of program implementation?

- How much time and energy will this take from our leadership team?

- What executive support do you need from us?

Other ways to prepare for this meeting include making sure you are knowledgeable about the leadership population in your organization (for example, what percentage of your leaders are estimated to retire in the next 5 or 10 years – an important thing to know to justify the importance of succession planning), and researching information available from leadership forums and human resource or development forums, to ensure your knowledge within the field of leadership development and succession planning is current.

Sample Presentation Slides

The executive presentation in every company will be different, based on your culture, decisions, and goals for the program. But to help save you some brain time (it always seems like the hardest part is just getting started on a presentation), here are some "generic" presentation slides that you can use as a template for putting together your presentation. The data on these slides will need to be modified to match your program.

NOTE: It is unlikely that you would want to use all of the slides in this chapter for an executive overview – many slide options are provided to ensure a variety to select from. Choose 3-4 key points you want to make in your presentation, and focus on these points.

What is a Talent Review Process?

- **Assessment of leaders** (and potentially individual contributors) in the company based on their **past performance** and **future potential**

- The nomination and review process of potential **successors for leadership roles** in the organization

- The nomination and review process of creating a pool of talent for focused development – **high potentials**

- **Assessing key positions** in the organization to ensure strong talent pools for continuous strong performance

- Reviewing the **strengths, development areas, risk of vacancy, and potential career path** of leaders

---

What is Succession Planning?

- Identification of individuals who demonstrate the potential to fill an incumbent's position on a **temporary or permanent basis.**

- Identification of individuals who are **ready now** to fill leadership positions, and leaders who are perceived to be **ready in 1 or more years**

- Identification and follow through of **development actions needed to further prepare successors** for future new and open leadership positions

- **Identification of future leadership positions** and the competencies that will be needed to perform effectively as these positions become reality

What is the Business Case?

- **Reduction of Experienced Leaders:** Within the next 5 years, an estimated "y" number of leaders are expected to retire in our organization; in 10 years, this number climbs to "x"

- **Cost of External Recruiting:** Each year, we spend "$x" on external recruiting costs; this process will develop an increased number of prepared internal leaders

- **Retention of Talent:** To retain our competitive advantage and innovation, we must continuously work to retain and develop our top talent

- **Shorten "Time-to-Fill" of Leadership Positions:** Currently, our organization takes "y" days to fill a leadership position; by preparing pools of internal talent and successors, we can reduce this expense

What Are Our Competitors Doing?

- **Enter research data here to briefly describe what the competitors in your industry are doing for leadership and talent development**

- **Enter research data and results here regarding leadership and talent development data from Hewitt, the Corporate Leadership Council, SHRM, ASTD, and other leadership organizations**

What is the Program Cost?

- Cost of development **resources, materials, workshops, e-learning**, etc.

- Cost of any **vendors or consultants** you will be working with on the program

- Cost of **systems and tools**

- Cost of **personnel** resources

- **Total estimated cost** of the program

What is the Timeline?

- **Planning** Stage – Complete

- **Talent Assessment** and **Succession Planning Stage** – Enter Dates

- **Talent Review** Meetings – Enter Dates

- **Post Talent Review** Data Entry and Analysis – Enter Dates

- **Development** Phase – Enter Dates

What is Expected of Our Leaders?

- Each leader is expected to plan and discuss their nomination of successors and high potentials with their leaders, and complete the **Talent Assessment** tool

- Leaders at the (supervisor, manager, director, etc.) and above level are expected to participate in a **Talent Review meeting**

- **Leaders are expected to have a meeting with each employee** to discuss career interests and create a development plan with each employee

- Leaders are expected to **follow through with specific action items identified for the successors and high potential individuals** in their work teams

What Executive Support is Needed?

- **Hold leaders accountable** for the expected actions we just discussed

- **Communicate** the value and importance of the process to our current and future leadership growth and needs

- Ensure adequate **financial resources** are available for successful implementation of the program, and for ongoing development

We hope these slides will give you a nice boost in developing your own executive presentation, as you present your final plans to your sponsors. Depending on the level of detail your senior leaders expect, you may need to add more detail around the program goals, metrics, and action plans. Or, you may only have 5 minutes to make your case, so be sure to know your audience.

Good luck with your presentation!

Section Two: The Preparation Stage

Talent Assessment and

Talent Meeting Preparation

Preparing for Success

Now that you have established your Talent Review and Succession Planning goals and project plan, and you have gained consensus and collaboration on your plans with your Human Resource partners and senior leaders, it is time to put your process in place.

This section covers the phase in which you will communicate the plans to your business leaders, implement a talent assessment data entry process, and prepare your leaders for Talent Review meetings.

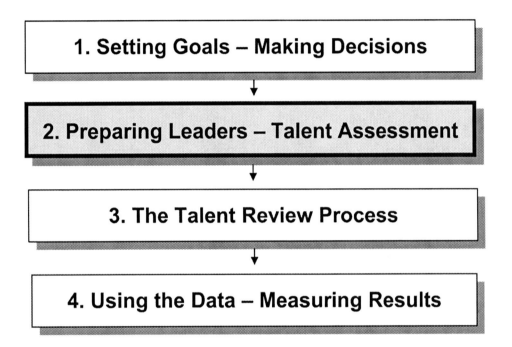

This section will help you make decisions regarding your talent assessment tool. In this section, we will also discuss methods for communicating the process to your business leaders. In addition, this section will help you prepare yourself as the leader of this process and as a facilitator of the Talent Review meetings.

What Questions Will Be Answered?

In this section, you will find answers to the following questions:

- ☐ To prepare our business leaders, what options and methods should be considered for our communication and talent assessment tools?

- ☐ What questions should I anticipate from the leaders, and what are potential responses to these questions?

- ☐ How do I schedule the appropriate amount of time for the Talent Review meetings?

❏ Who should participate in the talent assessment process and in the Talent Review meetings?

❏ What will be our agenda for Talent Review meetings?

❏ What will be the ground rules for our Talent Review meetings?

❏ What are my responsibilities as a facilitator of Talent Review meetings?

In this phase of the process, more business leaders and employees will be learning about the process, so be prepared for both positive excitement about the initiative, as well as concerns and questions that people will have. Make sure you are completely clear about the goals of the program, and connect regularly with senior leaders to ensure you have the support and alignment you need for success as you begin to roll out the program.

Chapter Nine

Preparing Your Leaders

Now that you have created your talent assessment process and tools, it is time to prepare your business leaders for their participation in the process. In this chapter, we will discuss ideas for what to communicate to leaders, and ideas for communication methods and tools.

In this stage of the process, you will also need to prepare yourself for the questions and concerns that leaders will pose to you. Questions will primarily pertain to the purpose and use of the talent assessment data, and to concerns regarding the creation of a high potential program (if you have included this as part of your Talent Review and Succession Planning process).

To prepare, you may want to review the chapter in this book titled "To Tell or Not to Tell", which provides answers to difficult questions you may receive. Remember, the identification of high potentials and successors is both an art and a science, just like virtually all other business decisions your leaders make every day.

During this stage of the process, remember to be flexible. Be prepared for some pushback on the process, especially if this is a completely new initiative in your organization, and be prepared to turn "pushback" into a "positive" by explaining the goals of the program and how it will help the leader run their business, retain their people, and develop their leadership team.

While you will need to make sure your process is consistent, and there will be some factors about the process that you can not bend on, there will also be times that you will need to be flexible in your plans. You may not be able to go with Plan A, and so you'll need to have a Plan B in your back pocket.

For example, if a financial leader says they can not start their talent assessment process this month because the quarterly financial statements are due to be completed, you will most likely have to schedule a later time for them to complete the talent assessment, or risk credibility due to a lack of understanding of their business needs.

Be sure to really listen to their perspective and their business concerns. Be open-minded to providing the best support you can for the unique needs of each business group. Be clear about what you can negotiate and what you need to be firm about, to ensure the corporate-wide consistency of the process.

Communication Tools and Methods

The communication tools you create for your leaders may vary in content, structure, and/or length, depending on your target audience. For example, you may need to create an executive overview presentation, have virtual or live kickoff sessions with mid-level leaders to provide time for questions, and create a mini e-learning module to be able to communicate the process to all supervisors.

Here is a full list of potential communication tools for your business leaders:

- A web site or Intranet page of information, Frequently Asked Questions & Answers, and access to your talent assessment tool

- Group kickoff sessions, including question and answer periods (provide food if you can – that always increases attendance)

- Leader's Guide booklets and/or Quick Reference Guides

- Executive Overview (presentation or documentation material)

- E-Learning Module that leaders can access and complete on their own schedule and refer back to as questions arise

- Attend as a guest at business group staff meetings to explain the process and to answer questions

- E-mail communications and reminders

Be sure to use multiple forms of communication throughout your process to ensure you reach all leaders and meet various communication styles and needs. Use different communication methods at different time points, to provide reminders to leaders in various ways.

It is also an excellent idea to include executive leaders in the communication process whenever possible.

For example, e-mail communications to all leaders regarding the purpose and importance of the process will be highly beneficial, demonstrating that your Talent Review and Succession Planning process is a corporate initiative, not an "HR initiative".

> *Be sure to communicate to everyone who will be involved in your Talent Review and Succession Planning process. Avoid reliance on a "trickle-down" communication method; instead, provide the communication tools directly to all participants.*

If an executive leader can be the opening presenter of a live presentation to leaders on the topic, this would certainly be advantageous. Or, include a cover letter from your CEO with any written document you provide to leaders. Working with senior leaders to present during one of their staff meetings also demonstrates their support of the process.

Communication Content

When designing your communication content, provide a very clear and concise step-by-step process, including:

- Discuss why the company is launching the Talent Review and Succession Plan initiative (it would be ideal for this part of the communication to come from your CEO)

- The specific goals of the process – what business results are expected?

- A definition of each stage of the process, and the leader's expected participation and actions in each stage

- A timeline of the process, deadline dates for actions to be completed, and each leader's specific time window, if applicable

- Clear definitions of each term you are using in your process, such as your definition of "learning agility", your definition of a "Ready Successor", your definition of a "high potential", etc.

- Instructions as to how to access and use the talent assessment tool you created

- An explanation of the confidentiality and security aspects of the system tools and the entire process, and how the data will be used

- Information about all leadership development programs in the company, and how the Talent Review and Succession Planning process, as well as a high potential development program (if applicable to your goals) is aligned with the company's overall leadership development strategy

- Information regarding who to contact for system-related questions and help

- Guidelines regarding an appropriate percentage of the business group population to be nominated as high potentials

- Information regarding who to contact for questions about the Talent Review and Succession Planning process

- Include a "Frequently Asked Questions" section, including questions such as:

  o If I can't complete the talent assessment process at one time, can I save my work and come back to it to finish later?

  o Can I nominate people who don't report to me as high potentials?

  o Can I select people who don't report to me as successors?

109

- o Who will participate in the Talent Review meetings?

- o What is the difference between the Performance Appraisal process and the Talent Assessment process?

- o Can any employee be nominated as a high potential? (You'll want to include any restrictions that your company has identified, such as a minimum time period of employment, exempt employee status, etc.)

- o Should I discuss my successor and high potential selections with my direct manager?

Preparing Participants for the Talent Review Meeting

You will need to prepare additional communications specifically for those leaders who will be attending the Talent Review meeting. This may be in the form of an invitation, a letter, or a memo. This document should include:

- The date, times, and location of the Talent Review meeting

NOTE: You may have multiple "levels" of meetings for different participants. For example, you may want to first meet with the most senior leader of the business group, to complete a Talent Review of his or her own direct reports. Then, these leaders will attend the meeting to complete a Talent Review of their own leaders.

If this is your situation, be sure to be clear as to when each participant should arrive. Also, allow some "cushion" time between these meetings, in case the first level meeting runs over time, and to provide a break for the senior leader and the facilitator(s) of the meeting.

- What to bring to the meeting, and/or how to prepare for the meeting

- The importance (or requirement, depending on your company) of having the Talent Review as a face-to-face meeting.

    NOTE: Having the Talent Review meeting as a face-to-face session is important because of the confidentiality of the discussions (it is impossible to know who could be listening when your meeting attendees are participating virtually), due to the richness of the discussion and the attention span you will need, and due to the length of the meeting. Our recommendation is to require the Talent Review meeting as a face-to-face session.

- The confidentiality of the meeting discussion

- General information about the topics / agenda of the meeting

- Include the "What's In It For Them" aspect of the meeting – what value will they obtain from participating in the Talent Review meeting?

- Additional "comfort" details such as appropriate dress, any meals to be provided (many business groups may want to include a team dinner before or after their Talent Review meeting)

Depending on your organization's culture, geographic spread, and size, you may want to establish your Talent Review meeting dates and locations at least 4-6 weeks in advance, to avoid scheduling conflicts and to allow plenty of time for travel arrangements to be completed.

Final Thoughts

Be sure to allow enough time for this leader preparation phase to take place. A few days will definitely not be enough. Making sure the Talent Review and Succession Planning initiative is clearly understood is more than half of the "battle" of implementing this process, so you'll want to give it thorough time and attention.

And, if you are implementing a Talent Review and Succession Planning process for the first time in your company, this phase of the project will be your first "test" from the leaders, as many of them will now be learning about it for the first time, and they will therefore be expressing their concerns, questions, ideas, and opinions.

Don't give up – there may be times that you hit a brick wall, but just remember you are running an important marathon, so take a break, have some fun, respond to the questions and concerns, and get back into the race.

Chapter Ten

The Talent Review Meeting: Facilitator Preparation

The Talent Review meeting procedure has been defined, and now everyone is expecting you to schedule and lead the meetings effortlessly, efficiently, and effectively. This chapter will help you plan and prepare for the meeting.

Your job is to accurately predict and plan the meeting agenda, the ground rules, and the appropriate length of the meeting. You will also need to compile and prepare data and/or documents that will be used during the meeting, and review the talent assessment data prior to the meeting to identify questions and concerns you will want to bring up during the meeting.

Review the Talent Review meeting goals you identified earlier in this book to create a written agenda for the meeting. Providing a clear agenda for the meeting will help keep the meeting on track, and will help ensure all participants understand the objectives and process flow of the meeting.

Make sure the agenda includes all specific talent review categories that will be discussed about each individual, to help the talent discussion flow more quickly and easily. For example, if you plan to discuss the next potential career move, vacancy risk status, strengths, development needs, and relocation ability of each individual, list these items on the agenda so you won't need to continually remind the meeting participants of the areas they are expected to discuss.

> *Even though you will have a clear agenda for the meeting, be flexible to allow for the unique needs of the group. For example, the senior leader may want to "break off" of the agenda to discuss a specific business need that is related to the topic being discussed. Or, the team may find a significant leadership competency need that needs to be further explored and discussed.*

Setting the Meeting Ground Rules

Through personal experience, we have learned that having a written set of meeting ground rules, in addition to the meeting agenda, is extremely helpful. This "sets the stage" at the beginning of the meeting for effective and appropriate discussions, and helps avoid the embarrassment of having to discuss a participant's problem behavior in the middle of the meeting.

113

If you prefer, have the participants come up with their own ground rules at the beginning of the meeting, and add in any that you know are important as well. Note the ground rules the group discusses on flip chart paper and post it in the room, to refer to these later if needed. Or bring a prepared Ground Rules handout to review with the group at the beginning of the meeting, that they can keep in front of them throughout the session.

Ground rules will vary based on company culture and values, but some potential guidelines to consider include:

- How cell phones, laptops, blackberries, etc. should be handled during the meeting

- Using appropriate "HR language", such as discussing the worklife balance need that Joe expressed regarding his career, rather than discussing the two high school kids that he has that are currently restricting his relocation ability.

- Discuss the roles of each participant, such as the facilitator, note-taker, participants, observers, etc.

- Discuss the need to keep the meeting on track, while also capitalizing on important discussions regarding the team's future leadership needs

- Remind participants that the Talent Review meeting is a "snapshot" in time, and to avoid forming permanent impressions of an individual's behavior based on the discussions. Performance can change either positively or negatively over time.

> *Make copies of the meeting agenda and the ground rules on colored paper, to make it easy for participants to locate and refer back to these documents during the meeting.*

- Encourage participants to listen, avoid interrupting each other, and for all attendees to fully participate.

- Discuss the confidential nature of the meeting, and how the data discussed during the meeting will be used.

Determining the Length of the Talent Review Meeting

Calculating the appropriate length of each Talent Review meeting is a balancing act between scheduling enough time to complete all of the agenda items of your meeting, while staying within the "meeting length tolerance level" of each of your leaders. And this tolerance level varies by leader, so you will need to get to know the expectations of each leader.

Even if this is the first time you are implementing a Talent Review and Succession Planning process in your company, you may have leaders who have participated in this type of activity in other companies, which is another reason to find out what the business leaders need and expect.

As discussed previously, we highly recommend that you require the Talent Review meetings to be face-to-face, for the following reasons:

- To maintain confidentiality – in a virtual meeting situation, it is impossible to tell who might be able to hear meeting conversations, or to know if each participant is in a closed-door location.

- To obtain the rich discussions and the concentration level you need. Conference call or even video conference meetings simply do not encourage the attention level needed.

- Typically, the length of the meeting is too long to be appropriate for a virtual meeting.

The length of each Talent Review meeting will vary considerably. We have personally facilitated meetings that were 2-3 hours in length and meetings that lasted for multiple days.

The three primary factors that will affect the timing of the meeting include the number of individuals to be discussed during the meeting, the number of components or agenda items you want to include in your Talent Review meeting, and the communication style of the meeting participants (and especially the communication style of the senior leader of the group).

Of course you will also need to factor in time for breaks and for lunch, if applicable. Build in enough time for breaks to enable leaders to check their e-mail and voice mail. If the leaders' tolerance level allows, it is ideal to be able to schedule a cushion of time (or to leave the meeting ending time open) to make sure you will be able to finish the meeting topics, especially if meeting attendees must travel to participate in the session.

Be sure to find out the flight arrangements of the participants, because they will leave when they need to in order to catch their flight, so it is best to know up front what your actual meeting schedule will be.

Keep in mind that the Talent Review meeting may be one of the few times the leadership team gets together face-to-face, and many groups also like to build in team-building activities or a dinner before or after their Talent Review session. If there is a choice, it is better for participants to have any team-building events or dinners before the Talent Review session, as they will typically be very tired after the meeting.

The chart on the following page identifies four primary timing factors of the meeting.

Four Primary Timing Factors

Timing Factors	Comments
1. How many individuals will be discussed?	Schedule 10-15 minutes per individual to be discussed. This factor can be significantly affected by timing factor #3 in this chart. In addition, schedule in time to review the agenda, ground rules, and for breaks, etc.
2. How experienced are your leaders at discussing talent?	If this is the first year you are facilitating talent review meetings in your company, expect the meetings to take longer. Once the leaders become comfortable with the format and content of the meeting, and they know what to expect, you can move through the discussions more quickly. You will see this "comfort level" increase during the meeting as leaders learn the "flow" of the talent discussions and begin to trust the process more.
3. How many agenda items will you be covering in the meeting?	You will want to time each separate component of the meeting to determine the overall length. For example, if your Talent Review meeting includes a discussion to finalize the high potential nominations, time this section according to the number of nominations to be discussed. If your meeting includes succession planning discussions, time this section based on the number of succession plans the group will be reviewing. You may also need to factor in how "old" the succession plans are; if they haven't been updated for a while, the discussions will take longer.
4. What is the culture and communication style of the meeting attendees?	Some people are just "talkers", and you need to know who they are. Especially if the senior leader is a "talker", this can significantly affect the length of your meeting. If you are not familiar with the communication culture of the work team you will be facilitating, talk with your HR partners or anyone else who is familiar with the group.

If this is the first time you are implementing a Talent Review and Succession Planning process in your company, expect some pushback on the length of the meeting. Remember that the participants have not seen the process before and do not automatically know what the value of this meeting is to them and to their business results. Explain the agenda of the meeting, and be prepared to be flexible (would it work better to hold two meetings of a shorter timeframe rather than having one long meeting?).

Here is an example of the timing of a sample Talent Review meeting:

30 minutes	Introductions, Agenda, and Ground Rules
30 minutes	Senior leader presentation of the group's business goals, the talent needs to achieve the goals, and the current open and future leadership positions
2 hours	Review the strengths, development needs, career potential of 12 leaders (10 minutes X 12 leaders = 120 minutes)
1 hour	Discussion of nominated high potentials to finalize the selection of these individuals
1 hour	Discussion of the group's succession plan
1 hour	Breaks and lunch throughout the session

Total: 6 hours

So this sample Talent Review meeting should be scheduled as an all day meeting, with flexibility around the starting and ending times depending on the group culture, flight schedule needs, etc. This also allows some "cushion" for additional people issues that tend to come up during the meeting, and for breaks that tend to run over time as the meeting participants are returning calls, etc. And of course, if you add additional agenda items to your Talent Review meetings, be sure to add time to your meeting to discuss these items.

Multiple Level Talent Review Meetings

When timing the Talent Review meeting, you will also want to consider how many different levels of meetings may be needed. For example, you may want to have a short meeting with the senior leader of the group, to discuss his or her direct reports, his or her succession plan, and any high potentials nominated who will be attending the next meeting. Then, the next tier of leadership comes into the meeting, and a second level meeting takes place. Typically, you will need at least two meeting tiers – one for the senior leader to discuss his or her direct reports before they come into the room, and one for the mid-level leaders to review the remaining leadership population of the group. The number of meetings you will need may also vary based on the size of the business group.

An example of a "tier meeting" process that could occur over a two-day period is shown below:

Meeting #1

Participant: Executive Vice President only

Leaders Discussed: Five Senior Vice Presidents

Time Requirement: Two Hours

Meeting #2

Participants: Executive Vice President and Five Senior Vice Presidents

Leaders Discussed: Twelve Vice Presidents

Time Requirement: Six Hours

Meeting #3

Participants: Twelve Vice Presidents

Leaders Discussed: 20 Directors

Time Requirement: Eight Hours

This example shows a "top-down" approach to the tiered Talent Review meeting process. The advantage of this approach is that the most senior-level leaders of the company or business unit begin the process by clarifying the talent needs of the organization, and by serving as a positive role model, demonstrating his or her value of the process by starting the process off themselves.

Another option is to reverse this order, having the supervisor or middle management level complete their Talent Review meeting first, and then continue to *roll up* the Talent Review data into higher levels of leadership, finishing with the top senior level meeting. This will provide an opportunity for the senior leader to complete a final review of all of the decisions that have taken place during the Talent Review meetings throughout his or her business group. In addition, this approach tends to provide more talent information to the senior leaders as they participate in their meeting, which enhances the decision-making process regarding the selection of high potentials and successors.

The Talent Review Meeting Environment

The meeting environment can be a surprisingly significant factor in the effectiveness of your Talent Review meetings. The list below includes some factors to consider if you have influence over the facilities that are selected to hold the Talent Review meeting:

- ✓ **The size of the room is important:**

    - o If the room is too large and participants are spread apart too far from each other, side conversations may start to occur, participants may not be able to hear each other well, and it tends to reduce the cohesiveness and energy level of the team discussions, particularly if the participants work in different locations and don't know each other that well in the first place

    - o If the room is too small, participants feel cramped and edgy, and this can especially be a problem if the session will be an all day meeting

- ✓ **Make sure you have the correct audio – visual equipment:**

    - o A projector for viewing employee profiles, presentation slides, etc.

    - o Internet connectors for meeting participants to check their e-mail during breaks (if desired)

    - o A flip chart for any "parking lot" items that come up that are important for the group but require a different meeting or action to address

- ✓ **Provide adequate refreshments for participants,** including coffee, water and soft drinks, and breakfast and lunch if appropriate (if the meeting runs over the lunch period, our recommendation is to ALWAYS provide lunch in the room or the lunch break will run too long)

- ✓ **You may want to provide "fidget items" on the tables** if the meeting length will be long, such as foam stress balls, to increase energy and help people focus on the meeting discussion

Preparing to Facilitate the Talent Review Meeting

If this is the first time you are facilitating a Talent Review meeting, be sure to read the Talent Review Facilitation Techniques chapter in this book. It would be ideal to have an experienced facilitator co-lead the meeting with you, whether this might be someone else in your company or an external consultant.

As the facilitator, you have the following role and responsibilities to complete as you prepare for the meeting:

- **Make sure you have the help you need to create a successful meeting – who will be attending the meeting to take notes during the discussions?** Who will be making the logistical arrangements for a conference room, food, audio/visual equipment, etc.?

- **Check the progress of the talent assessment data entries completed by the leaders prior to the Talent Review meeting to make sure all leaders have followed through on this responsibility.** Follow up with leaders who have not completed their talent assessment process. Attention to detail is critical to make sure the process is fair and consistently applied across the organization.

- **Prepare copies of documents you will need for the meeting,** such as the agenda, ground rules, list of individuals to be reviewed, list of nominated high potentials, etc.

- **Make sure the meeting participants have the information they need** to be prepared for the meeting discussions, and to make appropriate travel arrangements, if needed

- **Ensure the logistics of the meeting are all in place,** whether you do this yourself, or if you are able to obtain the help of one of your Human Resource partners or the business unit executive assistant.

- **Compile data and/or print reports from your talent assessment system prior to the meeting.** You may also need to create "overview" documents or graphs to provide a high level view of the leadership benchstrength of the business group. Make copies of data for the participants as needed for the meeting, and/or create online presentation material.

  You will want to have documentation regarding the talent assessment data entered by the leaders, the initial succession plans they created, the high potentials they nominated, executive profiles or resumes of individuals, etc.

  This type of information is especially important in larger organizations, where the Talent Review meeting participants may not know all of the individuals being discussed. Make copies of the agenda, ground rules, definitions, etc. that meeting participants will need to refer to throughout the session.

  If you are going to be discussing the same topics for a number of individuals to be reviewed during the meeting, it is a good idea to provide a list of these topics, before and during the meeting, to the participants. This helps them to be prepared with the information and to keep the meeting discussion moving along.

For example, if you plan to discuss risk of leaving, leadership ability, strengths and development needs of all leaders in the business group during the meeting, provide this list to the meeting participants prior to the session, so they can obtain this information about their direct reports, if needed.

VERY, VERY IMPORTANT

(This advice can prevent potential embarrassment and morale issues)

You may need to have different versions of documents for the Talent Review meetings, if you have multiple levels of meetings with different participants. For example, if you are passing out a list of nominated high potentials to the meeting participants for review, it's best not to have one of the meeting participants shown on the list! We've even had situations where a meeting participant was a spouse or other relative of one of the individuals being discussed. It is your job as the facilitator to review any documents that will be distributed in the meeting to avoid these types of issues.

What to Expect as a Talent Review Meeting Facilitator

Facilitating a Talent Review meeting, especially if it is a full day meeting, will be one the most exhausting things you will do in your career, so be careful about partying too much the night before the session!

All day you will need to listen very carefully, formulate good questions to encourage new perspectives and considerations, consider the unique business aspects of the group as you are facilitating, take notes (if you don't have another person attending as a note-taker), and continuously balance the need to keep the meeting on track while not interrupting valuable discussions.

- Bring fun items for the participants to fiddle with during the long meeting – i.e. stress balls, plastic springs, etc. This helps lighten the meeting atmosphere and increase the comfort level of the participants. If you have participants who are participating in a Talent Review meeting for the first time, they may be nervous or even somewhat suspicious about the process, and it is your job as the facilitator to help put people at ease.

- One or two days before the Talent Review meeting, review the talent assessment data and documents to identify issues, questions to bring up during the meeting, succession plan gaps, etc.

For example, if an individual has been nominated as a high potential but was given a low "advancement aspiration" rating by the leader, this would be a question to bring up in the meeting, to find out why the rating was low.

Typically, a high potential should have a high advancement aspiration rating, but there may be a temporary situation going on that provides the reason for the low rating. Or, you may find that the leader didn't factor in the low advancement aspiration when making the nomination. As the facilitator, you will want to provide some information or pushback on this nomination.

But remember, as the facilitator of the meeting, you MUST remain objective. As the facilitator, you should not provide your own opinions regarding the individual being discussed.

> *Remaining objective during the Talent Review meeting builds trust. As a Talent Review meeting facilitator, building trust is critical. You will have knowledge of highly confidential data regarding individuals' strengths, development areas, succession plans, etc. You must maintain trust to be an effective leader of this process.*

As the facilitator, it is your job to ask questions and push back appropriately if you see an issue, but ultimately the business unit leaders must make the decisions regarding their succession plans, high potentials, development action plans, etc.

If you break away from being objective, you run the risk of losing trust of the participants regarding how the data will be used, because if you are seen as modifying or changing the meeting discussion to match your own opinions, what might you do with the data after the meeting?

So what do you do if you are aware of a strength or development area for an individual being discussed during the meeting, and no one is mentioning it? Ask a question. Instead of supplying your opinion – "Katie has great presentation skills" – you can ask, "How would you describe Katie's presentation skills, which are important for this position?"

IMPORTANT: At the end of the meeting, be sure to review with the participants again how the data will be used, the confidentiality of the discussions that took place, any additional action items and what will happen next with the data discussed during the meeting. You may need to review specific policies, such as waiting until all Talent Review meetings have been completed to notify high potentials. Clarify that the leaders will be advised of the appropriate time to notify high potentials, and that they will receive "talking points" to assist them with the notification process (if this is applicable in your organization).

You Are Ready!

So you are now prepared for the Talent Review meeting, and you've prepared those who will be helping you with the meeting, and you've prepared the meeting participants so they know what to expect and what to bring to the meeting. Enjoy the Talent Review meeting day, be confident, and remember to be flexible and create a team-building environment.

Section Three: The Implementation Stage

The Talent Review Process

Gathering Talent Information

You've completed the quantitative part of the Talent Review and Succession Planning process, by asking leaders to use a consistent and objective talent assessment tool to review all of their direct reports. You have a large volume of data regarding the leadership talent in your organization, as well as nominated high potentials (possibly a very large number of individuals have been nominated for this program), and leaders have created initial succession plans, and discussed them with their own leaders. And, you've prepared your leaders and yourself for leading the Talent Review meetings.

This section covers the phase in which you move into the qualitative part of the process, where leaders of each business group come together to hear each others' perspectives on the future leadership potential within the group, to raise visibility of talented individuals in the group, and to review each other's succession plans.

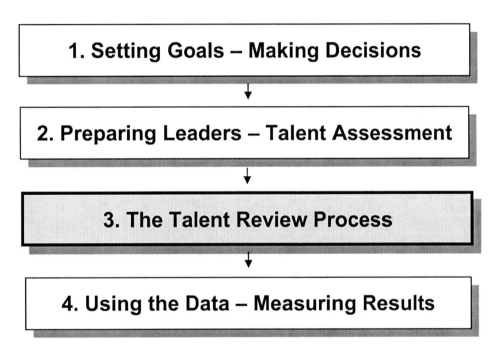

Both the quantitative talent assessment phase and this qualitative discussion phase are important parts of your overall Talent Review and Succession Planning project. Without the talent assessment phase, you enter the Talent Review meeting with a "blank slate", which would greatly increase the length of the Talent Review meeting, and would make it more likely that the more aggressive leaders will dominate decisions for the succession plans and the high potential group.

And, without the talent assessment phase, it is much more likely that some very talented individuals in the group might be forgotten, as you are then simply relying on the memories and the "favorites" of the individuals who attend the Talent Review meeting.

Without the Talent Review meeting phase, you have too much data, and you have data that is not necessarily agreed upon by all members of the senior leadership team. The Talent Review meeting provides a consensus forum, a learning exercise (what leadership traits do we value for our team, and what talent do we have for the future of our team?), and an additional step of the process to help validate selection of successors and high potentials, as the entire team has to agree on these individuals.

This section will help you facilitate the Talent Review meeting effectively, follow through on action plans after the meetings, compile Post Talent Review data, and notify high potentials, if this is component is part of your overall process.

What Questions Will Be Answered?

In this section, you will find answers to the following questions:

- ❏ How can I successfully keep the Talent Review meeting on track to complete the session objectives?

- ❏ How can I stimulate rich discussions during the Talent Review meeting to keep participants engaged, keep them thinking, and to present new perspectives, while staying objective?

- ❏ How do I notify high potentials to let them know they have been selected for this development program? What factors should I consider during this sensitive notification period?

- ❏ How do I obtain feedback from leaders and HR partners on our Talent Review and Succession Planning process?

- ❏ After the Talent Review meetings, how do I make the best use of the data? What actions should I take after the Talent Review meetings?

Be prepared for a lot of long hours during this phase of the project, but you can also look forward to a very challenging and interesting time in your career, and one in which you will learn a significant amount about your company and the people who make it successful. You will have an opportunity to meet many new people, and to help them learn more about their own organization, and help them plan for their future. Your own visibility in the organization will also increase, as you continue to meet with multiple senior and mid-level leaders through the company.

Chapter Eleven

Talent Review Facilitation Techniques

Leading a Talent Review meeting is a very interesting and challenging job. You will want to be thoroughly prepared, and always remember that it is important to stay flexible. This chapter will provide tips and techniques to help you successfully facilitate a Talent Review meeting. You have multiple jobs to do as the Talent Review meeting facilitator. We will discuss the following facilitator responsibilities in this chapter:

❑ Establishing and communicating the agenda and the ground rules for the meeting.

❑ Keeping the meeting on time and on topic, leading participants through the agenda items and categories of discussion, to ensure the Talent Review meeting objectives and agenda items are achieved

❑ Balancing communication styles and personality issues, and ensuring equal participation and discussion among the Talent Review participants

❑ Helping the meeting participants to look at people and issues in a new or different way, by asking questions and by appropriately challenging the way people are thinking, and by remaining objective during the discussions

❑ Using your Talent Review meeting documents to help the participants focus on the discussion and to understand the meeting structure and flow

❑ Taking careful and detailed notes in the meeting (or ensuring that another facilitator takes careful and detailed notes during the meeting)

Goal #1: Establishing the Agenda and Ground Rules

Your first objective as the facilitator is to make sure the Talent Review participants understand the overall purpose of the meeting, the specific objectives to be met during the meeting, and each person's role in the meeting. The three main components of the introduction section of the meeting include:

• The introduction of all participants (you may want to include an interesting icebreaker question to make this more interesting and to help participants become more comfortable with each other)

• Clarification of roles

• A review of the meeting agenda

- A discussion of the ground rules for the meeting

Introduction of Participants: Although most, if not all of the Talent Review participants will know each other already, it is a good idea to start with a very brief introduction and/or icebreaker to get things rolling. Use a simple introduction process such as everyone presenting their name and position along with something even close co-workers may not know, such as:

✓ Describe the most memorable teacher you had in school

✓ What food will you absolutely not eat?

✓ What is the best (or worst) movie you have ever seen?

✓ Describe a "brush with fame" moment you have experienced

Clarification of Roles: During the introduction, it will also be important to clarify roles of the participants. Who is leading and facilitating the meeting? Explain to the participants that the job of this person is to remain objective, ask good questions, and keep the meeting on track. Who is taking notes during the meeting? Who will serve as an additional "timekeeper" to notify the participants if the meeting discussion is going off track? Who is expected to participate and provide factual examples of leadership behaviors of those being reviewed in the meeting?

The Meeting Agenda: Be sure to have a written agenda document to distribute at the beginning of the meeting. Use this agenda to review the purpose and objectives, and to help the participants understand the timing and pace of the meeting to complete all objectives. Items on your agenda will vary, based on the decisions you made about the goals of your Talent Management process earlier in this book, but sample agenda topics may include:

o A presentation from the senior leader about the future leadership needs and competencies for the business unit, to help "set the stage" for the characteristics that are most important to think about for successors and high potentials

o Leadership positions that are currently open in the business unit, and/or potential future leadership positions that will be needed in the business unit

o Discussions of each leader (determine what leadership levels will be included in the discussions), regarding their strengths and development needs, where they may go next in their career, their perceived retention risk, their leadership ability, etc.

o Succession plan discussions to validate the plans, update the plans, or add to the plans o   Discussion and consensus regarding the identification of high potential individuals (your organization may still require executive approval of the high potential population following the Talent Review meetings)

o   A review of the "next steps" of the Talent Review process – how will the data discussed in the meeting be used, when should (or if) the high potentials should be notified, etc.

Ground Rules: Establishing group rules for the meeting, and providing these in writing (whether in a document or on a flip chart) during the meeting is extremely important, to avoid problems that can occur right from the start of the meeting. In addition, if problems due occur during the meeting, you can refer participants back to the ground rules. Examples of ground rules for your meeting may include:

- **Place cell phones and pagers on vibrate**

- **Avoid references to an individual's family life, medical situations, age, etc. – focus on job performance**

- **Use factual examples of job performance**

- **Think of recent behavior examples – situations that have occurred within approximately the last year**

- **Typically the individual's leader (if present in the meeting) will be the first to describe the leadership traits and abilities of the individual, but it is important for others who have worked with the individual to also describe what they have observed and experienced when working with this person**

- **Remember that all information discussed in the meeting should be used in a confidential manner, on a need to know basis. For example, it would not be appropriate to share the information discussed in the meeting with a peer from another business unit, but it is appropriate to share the strengths and development needs with the individual who was discussed in the meeting, to help them as they put together a development plan**

- **When discussing an individual, balance the important need to be specific and to provide enough detail, as well as being concise, to keep the meeting on track**

Goal #2: Keeping the Meeting on Track

The most challenging part of facilitating the Talent Review meeting is balancing the need to keep the meeting on track and on time, while also recognizing and encouraging rich discussions that will occur and need to occur. Your job as the facilitator is to ensure the objectives of the meeting are completed, to keep distracting side discussions from occurring, and to help the team bring up and discuss leadership strength and development need issues that are either helping the team be successful, or holding the team back.

One way to keep the meeting on track is to use your Talent Review documents that you prepared prior to the meeting at the appropriate time. Distribute these documents as you come to the appropriate point in the meeting – don't distribute them all at the beginning of the meeting, which can be overwhelming and can cause participants to lose focus.

For example, distribute the benchstrength document with the names of the individuals to be discussed, with any information you can obtain about the person prior to the meeting (i.e. length of time in the company and length of time in their current job position).

When the leaders have a document (or a flip chart or PowerPoint slide) in front of them with the information to be discussed, as well as the definitions you are using (i.e. what is a high potential?), the meeting will flow much more smoothly. This prevents you as the facilitator from having to continually prompt the Talent Review participants with each factor they should discuss as an individual is being reviewed.

To help you recognize whether the discussion should go to a "parking lot", or if it should continue because it is a key leadership issue for the team, or if it is producing no real value, ask yourself these questions:

- **Does this discussion impact the whole team?** If not, this may be a good parking lot question that a sub-team should take "offline" and discuss at another time.

- **Did the team just experience a big "light bulb" type of eye opening moment** in realizing a weak area of leadership benchstrength that did not occur to the leaders until the Talent Review meeting? If so, the discussion should probably continue.

- **Are the leaders getting into a business issue that does not pertain in any way to the objectives of the Talent Review meeting?** If so, the issue should go to a parking lot or the facilitator should ask the team to move on to the next Talent Review agenda item.

- **Are the Talent Review participants "beating a dead horse"?** In other words, has the point already been made multiple times? This most often occurs when team members feel strongly either about an individual's superior performance, or most often, if a poor performance issue has been observed by multiple team members.

  While it is important to have more than one "data point" regarding an individual's job performance during the Talent Review meeting, there are times the team could almost go into feeding frenzy of sorts in discussing multiple situations they have observed in an individual concerning a specific behavior issues. If this is the case, help the team to move on the to next agenda item.

- **Are cell phones, pagers, blackberries, or laptops getting in the way of timely, rich discussions?** Since this was discussed as part of your Ground Rules discussion, remind the participants that these side discussions and actions are impacting the objectives and timeliness of the meeting.

❑ **Is the team having a good cross-functional discussion** in which the business group leaders are learning more about the leadership talent in other parts of the organizational structure? If so, the discussion should continue, as this is an overall objective of the Talent Review meeting.

❑ **Are leaders disagreeing as to the validity of an individual as a high potential or as a successor?** If so, the discussion should continue, as it is important for the leadership team to come to consensus on this validity issue. If the team cannot agree, it is best not to confirm an individual as either a high potential or a successor.

❑ **Are leaders showing signs of fatigue by going off on discussion "rabbit trails" or going in circles with the discussion?** If so, give the Talent Review a break period; chances are very good that the team will be refreshed and ready to move on after the break.

❑ **Are leaders discussing the situation of a weak performing leader on the team that needs to move to a more aggressive step such as a performance improvement plan?** If so, give the team time to discuss the situation; most of the time, as a leadership team, these people discussions like this take a back seat in staff meetings to urgent business issues and project status reports, so many times the team has never before discussed together how the weak leader is impacting the team and/or the organization.

❑ **Is the team excitedly discussing the situation of a highly talented individual who is ready for a career move within the team or the company?** This type of discussion should continue. As with the situation of discussing a poor performing leader, this type of dialogue does not normally occur in regular staff meetings.

Often, the Talent Review meeting is the only time the leadership team learns about talented individuals (who don't report directly to them) and their skills and competencies that could also be highly valued in other functions with the team or company. This type of discussion encourages cross-functional career movement, which is one of the most important actions to take when developing talented individuals and leaders in the company.

The most important tools you have as a facilitator to keep the meeting on track and to ensure consistent discussions regarding each leader are your meeting documents. Continue to refer to your agenda, the ground rules, and documents that display the benchstrength discussion categories that help the participants move through the discussion of each individual.

Goal #3: Balancing Communication Styles

Another challenge you may experience while keeping the meeting on track and keeping everyone's interest is the challenge of balancing communication styles and needs. You will have Talent Review meeting participants who want to rush rich discussions and cut others off while they are making an important point, and then you will observe others who have a difficult time being concise in their communications and making a clear point. It is your job to balance these communication styles.

As the facilitator, you may need to assist when an important point was cut off by asking the individual who was interrupted to repeat or expand on what they said, and by indicating to the team that this is an important point. For the individual who is having trouble making a point, you may be able to help as the facilitator by succinctly rephrasing the point you think they are making, and asking them for verification to see if you are correct.

Goal #4: Asking Challenging Questions – Stimulating Rich Discussions

An important value the Talent Review facilitator provides is to help the participants think, and to see other potential perspectives outside of their own paradigms. As the participants are talking, your job is to think of other factors or issues that should be questioned. Some examples are listed below.

- **Ask questions to obtain additional critical information.** If the Talent Review meeting participants describe an individual as being at "high risk" of leaving the company, ask questions to find out what the risk is to the company if the person does leave (will it put significant strain on the work team, the business unit, or the company, or will critical knowledge and skills be lost?). You will also need to ask questions to find out what the strength of the succession plan is for the individual, and to determine if a more urgent and focused effort needs to occur in order to prepare any successors if the individual does leave.

- **Ask questions to pinpoint specific behaviors.** If a leader is described as acting more like an individual contributor than a leader, ask what behaviors are occurring. Does the leader stay in her office too much? Does the leader take on tasks for himself that should be delegated? Does the leader fail to take time to coach and develop people? Is the leader having regular staff meetings with her work team? Ask questions to pinpoint the specific behavior issues, to help you later in identifying development plans and resources for the leader.

- **Ask questions to obtain clarification.** Many times the descriptions you will hear about leaders will be very general, and you will want to ask questions to make sure you are clear about what the Talent Review participant is saying.

    For example, a common description you will probably hear is, "Sam has excellent communication skills." You may be thinking this leader has strong presentation skills, and what the Talent Review participant is saying is that Sam communicates well in meetings by contributing good ideas and asking good questions.

    Another common description is, "Casey needs to develop stronger technical skills." You may be thinking Casey needs a computer class, while the Talent Review participant is thinking Casey needs more knowledge of the telecommunications industry. Ask questions to make sure your understanding and your Talent Review documentation is accurate.

- **Ask questions to determine the impact of a leader's behavior.** Sometimes the Talent Review participants can accurately describe a leader's actions but not see the ramifications of these actions on the work team, on productivity, on employee retention, etc.

For example, if a Talent Review participant describes a leader in the Sales organization as having a communication style that is too abrupt or direct at times, probe to find out how this is affecting employees (is there an employee retention issue?), or customers (is this leader's style affecting customer sales, or is the leader able to modify their style in the customer arena, but not in the workplace?).

You will find that there are times an unproductive leadership behavior has been tolerated for a long time because others on the team have never discussed as a group how the leader's behavior is impacting the whole work team and business results.

- **Ask questions to help participants see another perspective or the "bigger picture".** Sometimes you will need to ask questions or to repeat something that was stated earlier, to help the participants see something you may be seeing.

For example, a Talent Review participant may be discussing a candidate as an Executive High Potential, citing the individual's strong business acumen and intelligence. As you look back at the notes you've already collected on this candidate during the meeting, you notice that the individual only has a few years of management experience, managing a very small team.

As the facilitator, you may decide to ask questions about the readiness of the individual to manage the larger business groups an Executive High Potential would be expected to take on. Or, you might probe into the individual's business acumen to determine their level work experience with profit & loss and budgeting responsibilities.

You might also ask if the leadership team feels the individual has had enough visibility and exposure to the executive team, who will be reviewing and confirming the candidate's selection as an Executive High Potential, to make it probable enough that the individual will be viewed as a high potential at this level.

Depending on the answers to these questions, as the facilitator, you may perceive the individual is a strong candidate for the high potential program, or you may decide to "push back" on the nomination, summarizing for the Talent Review team what you've heard, and recommend the individual be considered for other development programs or actions, until they can gain the experience, competencies, and visibility that will make them a stronger high potential candidate.

- **Ask questions to help participants identify how a leader's strength can be better leveraged.** Be sure to focus on the strengths of the leaders in the business unit, and not dwell only on development areas.

For example, let's say a leader is described as being an excellent coach and trainer for new employees on the team. You could ask questions to find out how this strength is being leveraged – is the individual conducting presentations for employees in the business unit to increase the knowledge of the work team? Would this individual be a good project lead for the competency model initiative that the team is considering? Would this individual be a good mentor for another leader on the team with a coaching skill gap?

- **Ask questions to find out the "why" behind the statements.** Sometimes Talent Review participants will expand on their comments appropriately, and other times they need to be "coaxed" by the facilitator to obtain enough information to determine if specific actions need to be taken.

For example, if the Talent Review participant says leader is at a "low risk" of leaving the company, ask, "Why do you think that?" If the Talent Review participant says the individual is ready for a career move, find out why. If the Talent Review participant says the individual is not viewed positively across all business units, found out why this has happened.

- **Ask questions to find out what actions have already been taken to develop the individual, and what the individual's career and development goals currently are.**

Sometimes you will need to find out what actions have already occurred to leverage an individual's strengths or to develop a weak area, in order to identify the next follow up action, or to obtain a more accurate picture of the individual being discussed. Here are some examples:

✓ If a Talent Review participant is commenting that an individual's leadership skills in the area of delegation and coaching need to be improved, ask what type of management training the individual has already completed, to find out if the behavior is more likely to be a knowledge and skill deficit or a motivational or communication style issue.

✓ If the Talent Review participant says the individual is ready for a career move, ask about career discussions that have taken place, and what the individual is interested in and ready to move into. Find out what the individual has already done in their career previously, and what competencies he or she demonstrates that could lead to a transition into another role or department.

✓ If the individual is experiencing a performance issue, ask how if the individual has been open to the leader's feedback on the issue, and if the individual is demonstrating a desire to improve in this area or not (this is also a "nice" way of determining if the leader has actually provided any feedback to the individual on this behavior, or if a coaching session is the follow up action that needs to take place.)

Goal #5: Remaining Objective

If you are facilitating the Talent Review meeting as an internal practitioner, you will probably know some of the leaders (who are being discussed) personally. *It is important to remain objective as a facilitator at all times.* If you begin to participate in the meeting by describing what you know about the person being discussed, you risk:

- ❑ Losing the trust of the Talent Review meeting participants that you will handle the information being discussed in a confidential and appropriate manner, without skewing the results later on to match your own opinions

- ❑ Losing focus on your responsibilities as the facilitator of the meeting

So, what should you do if you are aware of either a strength or development area of the person being discussed that you think is important, but no one has brought it up yet? Remember that your job is to remain objective and to ask challenging questions.

Let's say you have personally observed the leader being discussed in situations where he or she did not handle conflict well. Instead of sharing the information about this observation, ask the Talent Review team, "How would you describe the interpersonal skills of this individual?" or, "How does this individual handle conflict situations?"

Unless the behavior you observed was an "untypical" behavior for the individual, chances are high that others will also have observed the behavior and will now be able to comment on it. If this does not occur, then move on to another question or topic and resist the temptation to act as a participant of the meeting rather than the facilitator.

Goal #6: Identify and Discuss Potential Follow Up Actions

As you are listening to the discussion of each leader, you will also want to be thinking about potential follow up actions and development ideas for the leader, based on the needs.

Remember that the discussions that take place may "surface" very talented leaders that are not being leveraged as much as they could be, and below standard performance may also surface during the meeting, so your recommendations will need to reflect a wide range of needs. Some examples of frequently used development recommendations include:

- Participating on a cross-functional project team to build industry knowledge, build cross-functional relationships, and increase visibility

- Identifying a mentor who has a strength in the development area of the individual

- Recommending a specific workshop or e-learning class

- Identifying a job rotational assignment

- Increasing or changing an individual's job responsibilities to enhance knowledge and skills

- Recommending a coaching session between the leader and the employee, to discuss career interests, a development plan, or to provide feedback on a strength or development area

- Reviewing a very valuable and very "high risk of leaving" individual's compensation plan, if applicable

- Meeting with Human Resources to discuss a promotional opportunity for a high performing employee

- Placing the individual on a performance improvement plan

- Recommending a 360 feedback process for an individual who would benefit from learning the perspectives of others regarding his or her performance, as well as from a 1-on-1 coaching and development plan session with a 360 coach

- For senior level leaders, sometimes the best recommendation is to discuss the idea of using an external executive coach to develop a person for a high level leadership position, to help the leader with a transition period, to accelerate the development of a high potential leader, or to help a leader with a potential "fatal flaw" performance issue that could derail the leader's career if it is not addressed

Goal #7: Capturing Accurate Talent Review Meeting Notes

When you leave the meeting, your responsibility as the facilitator is to have captured all of the participants' decisions made during the meeting, as well as taking careful notes of their comments during the benchstrength discussions, all updates to their initial business unit succession plans, etc.

Some facilitators may prefer to take notes as they are leading the meeting, to help them to focus on the discussion. Other facilitators may prefer to have another person in the meeting take notes, to help them focus entirely on listening and asking challenging questions.

Our recommendation is to have more than one person take notes during the meeting, if at all possible. Sometimes discussions and decisions move at a very rapid talking speed, and it is difficult to document at this pace, so it is helpful to compare notes with another facilitator after the meeting. Even when two people are taking careful notes in a meeting, you will probably find after the meeting that each has captured different bits of information throughout the session.

You will also need to decide if the note takers will document the notes on a laptop, or if they prefer to take notes by hand. This will most likely depend on their typing speed (remember that the discussions can move along quickly).

It is perfectly appropriate for either the facilitator or the note taker to ask for clarification, or to briefly repeat back what was written in the notes from time to time to check for accuracy. This also helps the participants feel more comfortable, by hearing that their discussions are being captured accurately.

There will be many times that you will need to adjust the notes to be more appropriate, while not changing the gist of what is being stated. For example, you may document in the notes "Needs to increase professional maturity" for an individual who is described as being "high maintenance" or immature in some manner.

Question: Should I use a Tape Recorder to Capture Notes?

We don't recommend using a tape recording instrument in the meeting to capture notes, for the following reasons:

- The presence of a tape recorder may cause the Talent Review participants to be more uncomfortable being honest in their statements

- Even though you will review ground rules concerning the need to use appropriate on-the-job behaviors and avoid discussing an individual's family situation, or a medical condition, or referencing someone's age, it is still going to happen, and you probably don't want this type of comment recorded

- Tape recording the notes will mean that someone is going to have to listen to hours of tape, some of which will not need to be documented at all. Someone will need to spend time transcribing the discussions into a computer document later on (does anyone want to spend many hours doing this?)

- You can't really "see" if a recording is taking place correctly, and *what if a problem occurred and you found out later that some of the meeting conversations were not recorded?* You do not want to have to go back and tell the meeting participants that the notes were lost from the meeting.

Taking notes during the Talent Review meeting sounds like a "menial" job to some, but it is actually a very critical role that must be fulfilled by someone who demonstrates a detail orientation, who will fully understand of all of the conversation that will be taking place, and who has the trust of the Talent Review participants to record notes accurately and to treat the information with the highest level of confidentiality.

One Last Facilitator Tip (Okay, Maybe Two More)

If you are about to facilitate your first Talent Review meeting, be prepared for a very interesting day, and be prepared to be "on your toes" all day. Be sure to get enough rest the night before, and don't be surprised if you are incredibly tired when the meeting is over.

As you are facilitating the Talent Review meeting, you will be using a lot of "mind energy" leading the meeting. You will be listening carefully, thinking of challenging questions and how to ask them in a clear and appropriate way, taking notes during the discussions (unless you have someone else in the meeting take the notes), and watching body language for what is not being said (for example, you can see when participants are getting tired and they need a break).

IMPORTANT TIP: It is not a great idea to schedule your travel "tightly" when you are facilitating Talent Review meetings. For example, if you are facilitating a 1-day Talent Review meeting that is scheduled to end at 5:00, don't even try to schedule your flight out for that evening. If the group needs a little more time to finish the meeting, you don't want to seem like you are rushing, and you certainly don't want to leave the meeting without accomplishing the goals.

Also, don't schedule Talent Review meetings in different cities on consecutive days – provide travel time in between the Talent Review meeting dates. Trying to facilitate an all-day meeting, then catching a flight that night to another city, and then setting up early the next day and facilitating another Talent Review meeting is not a great idea. If your flights don't occur exactly as planned, you risk not even being there for the meeting. Considering the cost of bringing together multiple senior level business unit leaders for a day, it is important not make sure you are there both physically and mentally!

Facilitating a Talent Reviewing meeting is a very interesting job, and not one that many people have the skills and experience to do, so be proud of your accomplishment when your meeting has been successfully completed!

Chapter Twelve

After the Talent Review Meeting

Once you have completed the Talent Review meetings throughout the organization, you may feel that you just need a vacation. If so, take the vacation, and when you return, you will want to complete the three "F's" of the post talent review process:

- **Find out what they thought about the value and structure of the Talent Review process – evaluate and obtain feedback.** This will provide ideas for you to continuously improve your Talent Review process, and it will provide insight into the value the leaders of the company perceive the process provides for their business results.

- **Finish analyzing the Talent Review data – create charts, graphs, and development recommendations, and conduct Post Talent Review meetings.** These pictorial representations of the data make it easier for you to demonstrate and explain the results of the Talent Review meeting.

- **Follow-through on action plans as discussed during Talent Review meetings.** Out of everything you will do as you are planning and implementing the Talent Review and Succession Planning program, this is the most important, because this is where the business results happen, and this is where people change and grow in their careers and in their leadership effectiveness.

  You may be the one to help facilitate the follow-through actions during the year, or more ideally, this will be the responsibility of business unit level human resource or organizational development in your company, leaving you to focus on the overall company strategy, process, and use of the talent management process and data.

Who Needs to Know?

The data you obtain from the Talent Review process is incredibly rich information. But the value of the information occurs during the sharing and action processes after the Talent Review meeting. It is important for a variety of people in the company to review and analyze the data through a range of lenses – these people groups may include:

- Executive Leaders

- Business Group Leaders

- Human Resource Partners

- Recruiting Partners

- Compensation Partners

- Learning and Development Partners

- External Vendors (provide high-level development themes that resulted from your Talent Review process to enable them to suggest potential resources)

What Do They Need To Know?

You will also need to determine the most appropriate forum for communicating and discussing the Talent Review results with each group, as well as what type of information each group will be interested in. The chart below outlines some ideas on this topic.

Who?	What?	When?
Executive Leaders	<ul><li>Overall leadership population data and trends</li><li>High level, organizational-wide Talent Review results</li><li>Leadership Benchstrength data and recommendations</li><li>Succession Plans of Executive Leaders</li><li>Executive-level high potential leadership pool</li><li>What support and/or actions do you need from your CEO and/or executive team at this point?</li></ul>	Annual Executive Talent Review Session (at minimum)
Business Group Leaders	<ul><li>Business unit leadership metrics – i.e. ratio of leaders to employees, employee population data, etc.</li><li>Notes from the Talent Review meetings</li><li>Finalized succession plans</li><li>Development recommendations for the business group</li><li>Summary of action items</li></ul>	One session after the Talent Review meeting to review finalized notes, charts, + bi-annual or quarterly update meetings to review progress
Human Resource Partners	<ul><li>HR will need to access to all of the information and action plans for the business groups or locations they support</li><li>You may have specific action plans that are only appropriate for HR to follow up on; if so, be sure to specifically communicate these needs to your HR partners</li><li>You may want to provide a Talent Review overview session for your HR team, to present and discuss the "leadership state of the union" each year with them, as well as the action plan recommendations</li></ul>	Involve HR in all meetings you hold with the business groups or locations they support

Who?	What?	When?
Compensation Partners	• During the Talent Review meetings, compensation issues may be discussed, because they may pertain to a leader's "Risk of Leaving", or to a performance issue. Be sure to pass along this information to your Compensation Partners as appropriate.	As Needed
Recruiting Partners	• You will need to work with your Recruiting partners to determine what data they will have access to on an ongoing basis. For example, should all internal recruiters be able to view all succession plans? Should all recruiters be able to view high potential individuals? What about individuals who were identified as ready for a career move? • You may want to provide a Talent Review overview session for the Recruiting area that is similar to the presentation for the HR team, but includes a stronger focus on Talent Management and internal career development and movement	One session after the Talent Review meeting to review finalized notes, charts and plans, + bi-annual or quarterly update meetings to review progress
Learning and Development Partners	• If you have individuals in your organization who are responsible for organizational development, or for training within various locations or business group functions, partner with them to present your Talent Review data • Work with these individuals to share the Talent Review development recommendations and ideas that were discussed during the meeting, and to formulate plans and tracking methods for ongoing application and follow-through of the Talent Review actions.	One session after the Talent Review meeting to review finalized notes, charts and plans, + regular communication and meetings to review progress
External Vendors	• While you want to be careful not to share company proprietary information with external vendors, it is appropriate to share high-level development needs that were uncovered during the Talent Review process • Vendors can then suggest potential resources, workshops, and other solutions to work with you to address the development needs and leadership benchstrength issues to focus on in the coming year	One session after the Talent Review meeting to review finalized notes, charts and plans, + regular communication and meetings to review progress

With each of these audiences, you will need to view the Talent Review results from their perspective. Just like looking at a page of wallpaper in a book is very different from pasting it all over your walls, looking at your Talent Review data from an organizational-wide view can vary greatly from looking at your Talent Review data from a different

143

geographical site perspective or from a different business function perspective. Your job is to work with each of these groups and partners to take the data from a "pen and ink" resource and converting it into an actionable resource.

Be prepared for both specific questions (i.e. what do I need to do to enroll this person in the leadership development program you recommend?), and bigger picture questions (i.e. when will successors and/or high potentials be notified?).

Be prepared to update and change data from the original Talent Review meeting, if applicable. Recognize progress that the business group has already demonstrated. Address the most critical needs of the business unit to increase leadership benchstrength.

> *With all of the audiences you will be sharing information with, be sure to consider what is going on with that business group at that moment. What is keeping this leader up at night? What other projects and pressures are affecting the group right now? Remember to be flexible and to listen to concerns and external factors as you are discussing Talent Review results.*

What Information Should be Restricted?

First, you may want to check with your legal department at this point to determine if they have any advice or concerns regarding who is able to see what data from your Talent Review and Succession Planning process. They may want to formulate some type of confidentiality statement on any documents you produce that pertain to this data.

In addition, you will need to make decisions regarding who does <u>not</u> need to see or know specific information that resulted from your Talent Review and Succession Planning process.

For example, you will need to decide who can see the list of high potential individuals – maybe some individuals can see a partial list (i.e. the high potentials in the business units they support, or individuals who have been identified as being ready for their next career move), some individuals can see the entire list (we recommend that this be a very short list, as the more people who know something the more likely the information is to spread beyond the boundaries you would like to keep it in), and most individuals will not be able to view anyone on the high potential list.

We do not recommend announcing or posting the names of successors and high potential individuals in any type of public organizational forum, such as in a staff meeting or in the company newsletter. This greatly increases the potential issues that people are concerned about when it comes to identifying people in these categories, such as morale problems, or leakage of the names of these individuals to your competitors or external recruiters.

144

You will also need to decide who will have access to information such as individuals who have been identified as having a below standard performance level during the Talent Review meeting, individuals who have been identified as being ready to move to another position in the company for their development and growth, etc.

If you have a Talent Management system, defining security access to Talent Review data is a matter of setting the security levels appropriately for each screen and field on the system. This is a GREAT advantage of having a Talent Management system. Otherwise, you will need to "break up" your spreadsheets and documents from your Talent Review meeting into the pieces needed to be able to distribute the data to specific individuals or groups as needed.

Obtaining Feedback from Talent Review Participants

It is important to obtain feedback from the participants of your Talent Assessment and Talent Review process, to make continuous improvements that will make your procedures more effective and valuable to your internal customers. Some questions you may want to ask during your evaluation process, whether it is a survey, interviews, focus sessions, etc., include:

☐ To what extent did the communications provided at the beginning of the Talent Review process prepare you for the Talent Review meeting?

☐ To what extent did the tools and materials provided (list examples, such as a Talent Review Guidebook, online assessment system, etc.) prepare you for the Talent Review meeting?

☐ Did you receive the level of assistance and responsiveness you needed from your Human Resource partners?

☐ How would you rate the Talent Assessment process (provide specifics on the tools or systems you use during this phase of the project)

☐ Where the agenda and objectives of the Talent Review meeting clear to you?

☐ Was the length of the Talent Review meeting appropriate?

☐ To what extent were the Talent Review meeting facilitators prepared for the meeting?

☐ Did the Talent Review meeting facilitator remain objective throughout the meeting?

☐ Did the Talent Review meeting facilitators provide valuable insight, feedback, and questions to help you think about the talent within your business unit?

☐ Did the Talent Review meeting facilitators keep the meeting on track?

145

❏   To what extent was the time you spent in the Talent Assessment process and in the Talent Review meeting a valuable use of your time?

❏   Did the discussions and participation that took place in the Talent Review meeting enhance your relationship with your peers who also attended the meeting?

❏   To what extent did you learn more about the current and potential future talent that you have within your business unit?

❏   How confident do you feel that the actions discussed in the Talent Review meeting will be completed?

❏   To what extent do you feel confident that the information discussed in the meeting will be used in an appropriate and confidential manner?

❏   To what extent will the Talent Review process increase the leadership strength and future leadership candidate pipeline in our company?

❏   To what extent will the Talent Review process enhance the career development and opportunities for all of our employees?

❏   How critical are these Talent Review processes to the goal of building a future leadership pool in our company?

❏   Overall, what was the most valuable aspect of the Talent Assessment and Review process?

❏   Overall, what aspect of the Talent Assessment and Review process needs the most improvement?

❏   What other feedback or ideas do you have for the Talent Assessment and Review process?

Share the results of your feedback surveys, interviews, or focus groups with the appropriate partners, to increase understanding of what went well during the Talent Review process (remember to celebrate successes), and to work with your partners to make continuous improvements to the process.

Analyzing Talent Review Data

Before the Talent Review meeting, your job is to compile the Talent Assessment data into manageable documents that can be used for discussion during the Talent Review meeting. Then, during the Talent Review meeting, your job is to take careful notes to capture the details and accurate data that are discussed during the meeting.

After the Talent Review meeting, your job is to:

- Review the data, looking for trends and overall themes that pertain to the business unit

- Chart the data at an overall business unit (and/or company-wide) level, to provide the "bird's eye view" that senior leaders need to help shape their strategy and workforce planning

- Compare notes with any other facilitators or scribes who attended the meeting, to ensure accuracy and to obtain all details that were documented

- If you have an online Talent Management system, enter the data into the system and use the system to provide reports, charts, etc. (NOTE: It may be possible to actually document discussions in the Talent Management system during the Talent Review meeting. This saves you time later, and also enables the participants to watch the entry of the notes you are taking, to ensure accuracy.)

- Review the summarized data, charts, and graphs you have created; think of the discussions that took place during the meeting. Then, create an overall development plan for the business group, and create a summary of both the most urgent and important follow up actions.

  You might want to document follow up actions by category, such as the actions to address those who are at a high risk of leaving with high impact to the company, actions to develop those who are ready to move to another position, and actions regarding low performance issues that sometimes surface during the Talent Review meeting.

- Identify the strength of the business group's succession plan, and identify actions the department can take to develop successors and to be better prepared when current positions become vacant, and as new positions become available as the department grows.

> *Remember that a chart is just a picture of data – you will need to define the "so what" that pertains to the graph. For example, what if you create a graph that shows that 40% of the leadership population in a business unit is still "new" in their position – what does that imply? What if a chart for another business unit shows that 40% of their leadership population is ready for a new career move? It is your job to work with the business groups to help draw the conclusions and action plans associated with the analysis you have completed.*

147

As you are identifying development plans for each business group you will be meeting with, consider multiple options and be creative in your recommendations. Some examples of ideas and actions to consider include the following:

- If the group has a small percentage of prepared or ready successors, do they have a strong pool of successors who could be ready in one or more years? If so, what actions can be taken to expedite their development and readiness level?

- Are there individuals in the organization with specific strengths who can mentor another leader with a development plan in this area? Can business units with different strengths help and collaborate with each other to strengthen both groups?

- What actions do you recommend for the senior leader in the coming year?

- Is there a specific job function in the business group that has a weak succession pool?

- Do leaders in the business group need to get to know the career interests, backgrounds, and relocation interests of their employees better?

- Is the leadership to employee ratio too high or too low?

- Are there new leaders in the organization who need basic management training?

- Are there experienced leaders in the organization who will be transitioning into higher and broader leadership positions who could benefit from an executive coaching experience to increase the speed and effectiveness of this transition?

There are many more development plan recommendations available than we could ever list here. The point is to treat each business group, whether you are working with groups by location, by functionality, or by customer market, as the unique organization that they are, within the larger company.

Take time to think through and prepare your development recommendations prior to meeting again with each business group or senior leader. Even though you may be an internal practitioner in your organization, this is the time to put your "consultant" hat on and view the data and development needs as an external coach would.

Facilitating a Post-Talent Review Meeting

Once you have compiled the Talent Review data, created overall charts and graphs that depict the data, and you have written a development action plan for the business group, we recommend that you meet with the senior leader of the business group to review these results and action plans.

If you have an online Talent Management system, work with the leader to review the results you have compiled. If not, you may want to create a hard-copy document to review with the leader during the meeting, and for the leader to keep to track follow up actions and succession plan data.

The Post Talent Review meeting has multiple purposes:

- To review the Talent Review notes and data with the leader to ensure accuracy

- To provide a high-level view of the leadership strengths and development needs for the business unit senior leader

- To provide another reminder regarding the importance of following up on the action plans discussed in the Talent Review meeting, and building accountability into the follow up actions

- To reconfirm the accuracy of the high potential list of individuals, and the successors

- To review the development action plan you created for the business group

- To make any changes that have occurred since the Talent Review meeting took place

Typically the Post Talent Review meeting only requires 60-90 minutes of the executive's time, if you have spent considerable time preparing the data, graphs, and development recommendations prior to the meeting.

Follow-Up Meetings Throughout the Year

It is important to keep the development action plans in front of the business group leaders throughout the year, or the data will become "stale" and forgotten. The last thing you want to create is a Talent Review process that is viewed as an "annual activity" that "sits on a shelf" the rest of the year.

Ideally, you (or other Human Resource partners) will work with the business unit leaders at least mid-year or on a quarterly basis to review development plan progress, changes in the succession plan, etc. This increases accountability and follow-through of the important actions the business unit leaders identified during the Talent Review process.

It is best if you can obtain agreement as to the frequency of these types of Talent Review follow up meetings with the senior leader at the beginning of the Talent Review process. Compliance with these follow up meetings increases if you can "weave" it into other business meetings the group has already established, and making this type of discussion part of their business unit culture and routine processes.

You can also expect accountability and follow-up action to increase each year, as you continue your Talent Review meetings and development actions consistently over time. Leaders will come to expect and more fully understand the process. They will begin to think differently, and their understanding of the talents, work experience, career interests, strengths, and development needs of the individuals who report to them will increase.

Just as with any new human resource or business initiative, it normally takes at least a few years for the Talent Review and Succession Planning process to truly be integrated into your culture and leadership skill set.

Chapter Thirteen

Notifying High Potentials: Communication Ideas

The content of this chapter provides information and ideas to help you with the initial communications with leaders of high potential employees, and with your initial communications with the high potential employees themselves, if your organization has elected to notify high potential employees.

In addition, this chapter includes ideas regarding a "de-notification" process, for current high potential employees who have not been selected to continue in the program for another year.

Putting Together a High Potential Communication Plan

While there are many notification issues and questions to be prepared for, the benefits of retention and focused development for high potentials outweigh these risks. So, if you have now decided to notify individuals they have been selected to participate in a High Potential development program, the remaining information in this chapter will help you put together a communication plan that is designed to ensure leaders and employees have the information they need about the program, and to create a positive perception of the program within the company.

> *__Important:__ Ensure your notification process takes place __through__ your business group managers, rather than around them. Do not notify high potentials directly from the Human Resource department. High Potentials are selected by business group leaders – not by Human Resource leaders. This increases communication and the relationship between the leader and employee, involves the leader in the individual's development, and significantly reduces the error potential for notifying the wrong person, which you want to avoid at all costs.*

Your communication plan will require careful thought and planning. As with all well thought out plans, you will want to establish the goals you want to achieve from your strategy. Here are some examples of goals you may want to include for your communication plan:

- Goal 1: Managers and employees are aware of all leadership and employee development programs available to them – not just the high potential program.

- <u>Goal 2</u>: All employees in the company will have an overall understanding of the high potential program, and how employees are selected for the program each year.

- <u>Goal 3</u>: Managers will be able to answer questions they may receive from both the high potential participants and those who were not selected this time.

- <u>Goal 4</u>: Managers are aware of the high potential selection status of all of their direct reports.

- <u>Goal 5</u>: The most important goal is for the program to be perceived positively by all employees.

The First Element: People

The first decision is to determine who needs be <u>involved in and/or approve</u> of your communication plan; the following is a list of potential stakeholders who might fall into this category. Which of these groups needs to be involved to obtain their ideas and feedback? Which of the following groups will need to approve your communication plan?

- ❑ Human Resources

- ❑ Organizational Development and Training

- ❑ Corporate Attorneys

- ❑ Internal Communications

- ❑ Business Unit Leaders and Senior Executives

Next, determine who needs to <u>receive</u> communications and/or notifications. Your potential list includes:

- ❑ Your "Support System" – those who may be called upon to handle problems or questions that surface during the notification process (for example, Human Resources)

- ❑ High potentials participating in the program for the first time

- ❑ Current high potentials who have been "re-confirmed" to continue in the program for another year

- ❑ Current high potentials who have not been "re-confirmed" to continue in the program and will need to be transitioned to other development programs

- ❑ Managers of individuals in each of these categories – high potential participants and individuals being transitioned out of the program

❏ Managers who nominated an individual as a high potential during the Talent Assessment process, but the individual was not selected for the program during the final Talent Review meeting (or during the final Executive review process)

❏ All employees (if you decide to provide general information about the program to the entire organizational population)

Compile a list regarding the people who need to be involved, when to involve them, and what aspect of the notification process they will need to be involved in. Once you have finalized all plans for your notification process, be sure to facilitate a meeting with these individuals to communication the notification process, and to clarify what you are asking of them during the notification time period.

The Second Element: Systems- Processes - Resources

In this section, we'll discuss the communication tools you can use or select from to notify your high potentials. The communication tools outlined in this section include:

✓ A Talking Points Document

✓ The High Potential Notification Letter

✓ Marketing Materials – Corporate Development Programs

✓ Corporate Communications Media

✓ The High Potential Program Kickoff Session

For each tool, we'll discuss potential content, and provide "lessons learned" type of advice. It is important to customize these tools to the culture and needs of your organization.

A Talking Points Document

The first communication resource you can create is a "Talking Points" document for your leaders. This document provides an executive summary of the high potential program, the selection process, and the notification process. The document should be designed to help prepare leaders for potentially difficult situations and to answer these questions in a consistent, accurate manner.

Every leader in the company should receive this Talking Points document at the time of the high potential notification, even if they do not have high potential employees reporting to them, because any employee in the company may ask questions of their manager about the program during the notification period.

On the following pages are some examples of the content you might include in your Talking Points document. Of course, these will need to be customized to the philosophy and culture of your company.

❑ What is the High Potential Program? Provide a description of the program, including the purpose and goals of the program, why the company feels having a high potential program is important, the high potential categories (if applicable), and what percentage of the population is represented in the high potential group.

You may want to include benchmarking information from other companies who have similar programs, as well as data from leadership research organizations such as the Corporate Leadership Council, the Learning & Development Roundtable, and Hewitt Associates (Top 20 Companies for Leadership), to communicate this type of leadership development as a best practice for growing companies.

❑ What is a High Potential employee? Another potential piece of information to provide at this point is your company's definition of a high potential employee. Most (if not all) of your leaders should already be familiar with the definition through the Talent Assessment process, but it is a good idea to provide it again in the Talking Points document to ensure consistent answers to employee questions. This information can also be helpful to those who aspire to participate in the program, and it provides more information about the structure and selection process for the program.

❑ How are individuals selected for the High Potential Program? Provide a brief description of the selection process and how often the selection process will take place

❑ What can I do to increase my chance of being selected for the program next year? Encourage employees to have career and development discussions with their leader to identify strengths to leverage and development areas for improvement. If your company provides a 360-feedback process, include this as a recommendation to help identify these strengths and development areas. Encourage employees to participate in other leadership and professional development opportunities the company provides.

❑ Will the names of the High Potentials be announced? Provide your company's policy regarding this issue. The position we take on this is to not to communicate the names of the high potentials to your organization's population as a whole. There is little, if any, positive aspect to this, and it provides a detailed list of your company's greatest asset – your top talent – to your competitors and external recruiters.

❑ If an employee is asked, "Are you in the High Potential Program?" how should the employee respond? The employee should treat the question in the same way he or she would if asked about a salary increase or bonus amount. This information is confidential and should not be discussed between employees.

❑ If I'm not in the High Potential program, does that mean I won't be considered for advancement and development opportunities? This is a question that employees will be wondering, so leaders should be prepared for it. In most companies, it is true that high potentials have more visibility for promotional opportunities. However, all employees should have access to both advancement and development opportunities in the company - this is the place to provide descriptions of other leadership programs and development options employees can self-select for. Normally, the percentage of the high potential population is so small that it is very logical for employees to see that advancement opportunities will certainly not be limited to such a small group.

❑ <u>Do employees stay in the High Potential program indefinitely, once identified?</u> Of course this is one of the decisions your company needs to make, as discussed earlier in this book. Define your policy regarding this question. It is also important on this talking point to emphasize that employees who were not selected in the current year could be selected in the future, based on their performance and leadership potential.

One Communication Option: The High Potential Notification Letter

One option is to provide a notification letter for the manager to give to the high potential employee to congratulate them for being selected for the program, to include brief information about the confidentiality and "no guarantee of employment or promotion" statement, to briefly let them know what the program is about, and to tell them what to do next.

It is ideal to have your CEO or other senior leader sign the notification letters, if at all possible. After all, you are notifying typically the top 5%-10% of your organization's talent, and you want to convey the importance of the program.

WARNING: Providing a notification letter has some disadvantages as well – if you have a large number of high potential individuals, you will be creating a large number of customized letters. We also find that many times the managers don't give the letter to the employee. This can cause problems later on when employees find out that others in the high potential program received a formal letter, which results in frustration and concern about whether or not they were actually selected to be in the program.

If you have an online system or database that managers can access, you may find it to be easier and more effective to simply provide the "Notification Talking Points" to managers through e-mail, and direct the managers to the system to learn the final results of the individuals on their team who were selected for the program. This notification method puts the action and accountability on the business leaders, rather than on you.

However, you will still need to build in some type of communication method for the newly notified high potentials to contact you once their manager notifies them that they have been selected for the program. This enables you to begin communicating development events to them directly. One idea is to provide a special e-mail address for high potential employees to use to send a message that they have been notified and that they are ready to begin their development program.

If you do decide to create and distribute notification letters, here are some distribution ideas:

1. All of the letters can be delivered to the senior-most leader of each business unit, who can add a personal hand-written note to the letter before giving it to the employee. Senior leaders may want to hand deliver the letters to each employee themselves in a smaller organization, or the letters can then be delivered in either of the next two methods.

2. All managers of the company should receive a Talking Points document; managers who then also have high potential employees in their group can receive these employees' notification letters in the same packet. The manager would then meet with each employee to hand-deliver the letter (where this is possible geographically), and to congratulate the employee personally and hand him or her the letter.

3. Information about the high potential program can be sent to all employees and leaders. Then, notification letters can be sent to the employee's home addresses, with instructions to discuss the program with their leader after receiving the letter. This option may work well in a very large or virtual organization.

Another important piece of advice is to build an accountability plan for leaders who fail to provide the letter to the employee. It seems amazing that leaders would fail to notify employees about an important development program, but it can definitely happen.

Leaders are focused on business actions that need to get done, and some leaders will have some level of envy if their employee was chosen for the program and they were not, which could also factor into a delayed notification process. Have a plan ready regarding how you will handle this situation – by what date will this plan go into action, and what action(s) will be taken to ensure the notification process is completed within a period of 2-3 weeks, at the most.

> *A "lessons learned" piece of advice - build a methodology in your notification process so you will know when his or her manager has notified each high potential employee.*

Remember to customize each notification letter by name to each individual. The content of the letter may include:

*   A note of congratulations to the employee

*   Notification regarding which category of high potential they have been selected for (if applicable in your company)

*   A brief explanation of the program

*   A note regarding the confidentiality of the program

- A statement that the program is optional

- A statement that the program does not guarantee employment or promotions

- Information regarding what action to take next – i.e. registering for a Kickoff (introductory) meeting, starting a 360 feedback process, contacting personnel in Human Resources, etc.

Other High Potential Notification Methods

Using a notification process by hardcopy letters to leaders and/or to high potential employees themselves may not be the best solution for many companies, due to the size of the organization, the geographic spread of the company, the culture of the company, etc. Here are two more notification methods to consider:

- If you have an online Talent Management system that stores the identification of your high potential individuals with the appropriate viewing security levels, notify all leaders that it is time to go out to the system to learn which employees have been confirmed for participation in the program. Provide communication collateral for leaders to aid in this process, such as Frequently Asked Questions about the program, a Talking Points document, etc., and ask leaders to notify selected employees by a specific date.

- Some leaders may be interested in facilitating either a face-to-face meeting with their high potential employees, or a virtual meeting with their high potential employees to notify them. This provides an excellent opportunity for the leader to congratulate the employees personally, and to clarify his or her expectations regarding their participation in the development program provided.

Marketing Materials – Corporate Development Programs

In the notification packet to leaders, include marketing flyers or brochures that explain all of your corporate or leadership development programs. This emphasizes that all employees and leaders in the company will be developed – not just the high potential employees – and provides information leaders will need to help identify other programs, workshops, and learning resources for employees who were not selected this year for the high potential program.

Corporate Communications Media

Remember to use any existing corporate communication methods that are already in place to help communicate your program. Examples may be the company newsletter, an e-mail news process, bulletin boards, etc. These communication tools may be used to provide general information about the program to all employees or to all leaders.

The High Potential Kickoff Session

Facilitating Kickoff meetings (or introductory meetings) is the most important action you will take to help ensure the high potentials all get off to a good start. The Kickoff meeting should be the first development action your high potentials take, to learn about the program and what to do next.

The Kickoff Session is important because it provides:

- An opportunity to congratulate the high potential employees, and a chance for the human resource, organizational development, and or leadership development personnel to meet these employees

- Consistent messages to the high potential employees, regarding the value they bring to the organization, the confidentiality of the program, and the "no guarantee of employment, promotional, or continuation in the program"

- The materials, resources, and information the high potential employees will need to successfully participate in the development program

- An opportunity to meet senior leaders in the company

- A networking opportunity to build relationships with other high potential participants – the future leadership team of the company

The components and sessions of your Kickoff meeting will vary based on the development options you have chosen for your development program, but the Kickoff session might include:

- An overall introduction session to congratulate the participants, discuss the purpose of the program, how the participants were selected, and what the development program entails

- Planned networking events

- Sessions with guest speakers discussing specific aspects of the development program, such as a session on available e-learning resources, a session provided by your executive coaching vendor, a session on the 360 feedback process, etc.

- A session provided by your CEO or senior executives regarding the organization's strategy, leadership needs, etc.

- Learning sessions on leadership topics or competencies that are key to your organization

The Third Element: Costs

The costs involved in the notification process may include costs of the printing and mailing notification letters, Talking Points documents, brochures explaining your leadership programs, etc. In addition, you may incur costs for the "Kickoff Sessions" that may be minimal or extensive, depending on the content, facility needs, and extent of your Kickoff Session. These costs may include the printing and/or purchase of learning materials, audio/visual equipment, hotels (if applicable), travel costs, catering, facilitators, guest speakers, office supplies, etc.

The Fourth Element: Time

Because the high potential notification process is a very sensitive communication activity and must be handled carefully to avoid errors and miscommunications, it will take several weeks to complete the communication plan. Plan a timeframe of at least 6 – 8 weeks to complete your plan.

This plan does not include the time needed to hold Kickoff sessions – just the time needed to simply notify the high potential employees who have been selected for the program.

> *Ideally, plan a time period of 6-8 weeks to complete your high potential notification process.*

An approximate schedule may be:

2 – 3 weeks – Time to prepare your written notification and communication plan, and for key stakeholders to review and approve it.

1 – 2 weeks – Time to present the communication plan to your "Support System" personnel, such as Human Resources, Corporate Communications, etc. to enable them to support you and to answer business unit leader questions.

2 – 3 weeks – Time for business units to review their high potential lists, to make any final changes or to verify they are 100% accurate, before communications take place. During this time, you can be preparing notification letters and Talking Points for leaders.

2 weeks – Time for managers to meet with the employees who have been identified for the high potential program. At this time, you can ask the managers to give the notification letter to the high potential employee.

1-2 weeks – Time to follow up with leaders who have not yet met with their high potential employees to notify them. During this time period, high potential employees who have received their letters can be registering for the Kickoff Meeting of their choice.

The Fifth Element: Communications

Well, that's what this chapter is all about – communicating your high potential program in a well planned, structured way to accurately notify high potential employees, while taking care to ensure all leaders and employees are aware of the program and see it in a positive way. The keys to successful high potential notification include:

- Allowing enough time for the communication process – ideally, 6-8 weeks

- Involving your primary stakeholders, senior leaders, and "Support System" (such as Human Resources and Corporate Communications)

- Using multiple communication methods and media to ensure the message is comprehensive and consistent throughout the company

- Providing Kickoff sessions for high potential employees to attend to learn about the program, what to do next, and to network with other participants in the program

- Ensuring the accuracy of your high potential lists by double-checking with leaders and human resources to approve the list for each business unit

- Providing information for leaders regarding the high potential program, as well as all other corporate and leadership development programs available, to ensure they are prepared to answer questions employees may have

What About "De-Notification"?

Unless your high potential development program allows individuals to stay in the program indefinitely (not something we recommend), at some point individuals who are currently in the high potential development program will need to be notified that they have not been selected to continue in the program for the coming year.

There are many reasons that an individual will not be selected by their leadership team to continue in the program for another year. It may be that the individual has just moved from an individual contributor position to a leadership position, and now they need the organization's beginning leader development program, rather than the high potential program. There may have been a change in the individual's performance. There may have been a change in the leadership competencies needed to achieve the organization's business goals, due to a merger, or due to a period of intense organizational growth, or due to a change in the company's scope or direction.

Or, because most organizations limit the size of the high potential employee population, the company or a business group may simply think a current high potential employee has already gained the maximum value from the program, and decides to provide an opportunity for another employee to now be selected for the program in his or her place.

Here are some ideas around the "de-notification" process:

- The number one, most important, best way to prevent the potential morale issues associated with de-notification is to address this issue up front with all new high potential employees, during the Kickoff Session, as described earlier in this book.

Take the opportunity in this first communication session with high potential employees to make sure they know that they have been selected for one year (or whatever your company's time period is between high potential talent assessment and selection periods).

Advise these individuals to fully use this year to focus on their career and development needs. Discuss the fact that individuals will be re-evaluated each year (again, modify this based on your company's needs) and that the high potential population will change over time.

Emphasize that participating in the high potential program is not a permanent situation, and that when the time comes for another employee to take their place in the program, this should not be interpreted as a reflection on their value or contribution to the organization.

- Develop a tool or method of documenting the reason an individual is being removed from the high potential program – to be completed by the leader of the high potential employee, or by the individual who has made the decision to remove the employee from the program. This practice will help reduce risk of litigation issues because the process is consistent and the reasons are documented.

  In addition, this practice provides data you can use to measure the reason(s) individuals are removed from the program, which may be helpful if you decide to modify or update your definition of high potential employees for the talent assessment process.

- Provide some type of "Talking Points" and/or coaching assistance to leaders who will need to "de-notify" high potential employees. This will help reduce the likelihood of leaders making problematic statements as they are de-notifying employees, and will increase the comfort level and confidence leaders have as they are preparing to have this discussion with employees.

- Encourage individuals who have been de-notified to continue with their development. Emphasize the importance of continuing to follow through with any remaining actions on the development plan they created while they were in the high potential program, and communicate other development programs that are available to leaders that they can participate in to continue in their knowledge and skill development.

Remember: Patience is a Virtue During the Notification Process

One would think that the notification of high potentials would be an easy process – it sounds pretty straightforward. But our experience is that patience and a clear notification process is <u>critical</u> during this time period.

Rushing the notification process, or lacking a clear plan around how it will work can result in incorrect notifications and errors – clearly something you want to avoid at all costs to maintain the integrity of the program and to avoid any conversations that might start with the phrase, "I'm sorry but you are not really a high potential employee."

So remember the value of persistence when it takes a long time for a leader to notify an employee, and remember the value of attention to detail when preparing and organizing your communication tools, documents, and processes. And, to keep yourself motivated, remember how excited, proud, and valued people feel as they are being notified as a high potential employee!

Section Four: Measuring Results

Making It Matter

Gathering Talent Information

Great job! You've planned and implemented a Talent Review and Succession Planning process in your organization. This is a huge task and you (and your team or partners) should be very proud of the work you have done. Don't forget to celebrate your success!

Remember that the success of a talent management strategy is a journey. You may be able to measure and communicate some business results from the process early on (such as an increase in internal leadership career movement). Other results may take multiple years to measure effectively (such as preparing leaders for top executive roles).

Now it's time to demonstrate to the rest of the organization the value and business results achieved through your Talent Review and Succession Planning process. Although this section is towards the end of the book, your metrics decisions and data gathering actions should take place before, during, and after your program is implemented, as a continuous-loop process.

This section includes ideas for what metrics your company can use to measure the results of your program, as well as ideas for increasing accountability and completion of Talent Review follow-up actions. This is the time to reflect on the challenges or business needs that provided the initial catalyst for the implementation of your talent management strategy, to determine if those challenges have been addressed and if the business needs have been met.

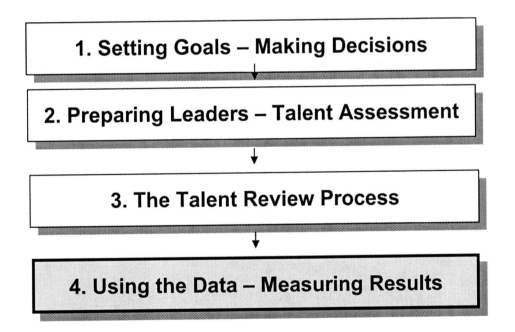

For many people in the field of organizational and leadership development, consistently measuring the results of the programs, products, processes, and services they implement is an ongoing challenge. It can be difficult to take the time to gather and analyze the data needed to measure business results. Our hope is that this chapter will help you streamline and organize the metrics planning and implementation process for your Talent Review and Succession Planning program.

What Questions Will Be Answered?

In this section, you will find answers to the following questions:

❏ What data is already available in my organization that may be used to help measure our Talent Review and Succession Planning program?

❏ What metrics should we consider when creating the evaluation plan for our program?

❏ For each metric, how often should we gather the data and review it?

❏ In our organization, who can provide the data we need, or how can we create a process or method of obtaining the data we need?

❏ How can we increase the accountability of our leaders to follow through on development action plans identified during the Talent Review process?

❏ How can we increase our own accountability to follow through on obtaining and analyzing metrics to demonstrate the business results of our program?

Use the information and the Metrics Checklist tool in this section during discussions with others in metrics planning meetings, or as aids while you are working on your own to form the strategy and data gathering processes that will be a part of your measurement actions. The format of this section is designed to enable you to customize your measurement goals and processes to the needs and culture of your unique organization.

Chapter Fourteen

Measuring Results

Just like the falling tree in the forest, our sponsors and business group leaders wonder if no one is there to measure it, did we really achieve any results?

Identifying metrics that align to the goals we are working to achieve, following through with measurement actions, and communicating the results to our sponsors, partners, and business group leaders are all essential components of the Talent Review and Succession Planning process.

In this chapter, we will discuss the following topics:

- **Creating Accountability** – Remember that metrics are just numbers unless you put accountability actions with them. Create a continuous loop of accountability and measurement. For example, work with your leaders to run quarterly metrics by business group – these should then "feed up" into a larger corporate scorecard. These results can also be used as part of the calculation for compensation rewards, such as including metrics for people development as part of an executive's annual bonus calculation.

- **Aligning Metrics to Original Goals** – In addition, we have a tendency to want to make sure the numbers always put our programs in the best light, so be careful about how you are "slicing and dicing" your calculations – any metrics can be made to "look good" or "look bad". Stick to your original measurement plan and goals to achieve, and be true to these.

- **Using Time Savers** – We also know and completely understand that measuring results takes time, so you will want to identify any resources, systems, or services that will help you track, use, update, and measure your Talent Review data. In this chapter, we'll provide some ideas and tips regarding the selection of the selection of software or a system to manage your talent data.

  Also, we will provide some ideas to help "spread the wealth" of the time it takes to measure results, such as involving partners and/or the participants of your development programs to identify and calculate metrics.

- **Communicating Results** – Remember to communicate results, celebrate accomplishments, and give recognition to development program participants who have achieved individual goals. We'll provide some ideas in this chapter around creating communication forums that are designed to both increase your own accountability (knowing that you have a communication device or forum deadline coming up and you need to have measurements ready), and the visibility of both individual and performance results in your organization.

After reading this chapter, your next step is to complete the Metrics Checklist that is included in this section. If possible, it is a good idea to complete the Metrics Checklist with others in your company who will be helping to provide data, helping to calculate data, and/or those who will be reviewing and analyzing the data.

Creating Accountability

To increase the follow-through and completion of Talent Review and Succession Planning action plans, which is the first step to following through with program measurements, you will want to create a structure of accountability for yourself, your partners, the participants of your development programs, your business group leaders, and your organization.

The table below outlines ideas for increasing accountability for each of these groups.

Accountability Table

Group Name	Accountability Ideas
YOU	• Create written goals and target dates for yourself and your team (if these are not already provided for you) • Create and communicate commitments to others in the organization that will then work towards (i.e. schedule dates for Post Talent Review meetings with leaders, schedule dates for presentations of overall Talent Assessment results to partners, etc.) • Create "progress tools" to update and circulate on a regular basis to sponsors and partners, such as charts that show all scheduled Talent Review meeting dates
INTERNAL PARTNERS **(For example, Human Resources, Information Technology, Organizational Development, etc.)**	• Include the names of your business group partners on the "progress tools" described above so each partner is aware of the status of actions they are also responsible for and how their actions impact others • Hold regular meetings to update partners on actions, results, and progress • Create written documents such as "quick reference guides", checklists, standard operating procedures, etc. and distribute to partners so everyone knows the steps of each process • Hold brief training sessions or "brown bag lunches" with partners to provide information; for example, you can hold a "mock talent review" meeting so everyone can see what occurs during the meeting and how to prepare for it

Group Name	Accountability Ideas
DEVELOPMENT PROGRAM PARTICIPANTS	• Ask participants to meet with their manager to discuss their development plan, and then provide a final copy of it to your department (or to enter their plan into an on-line system, if applicable) – provide a specific due date for this action to be completed • Hold the "Kickoff Meetings" described earlier in this book to explain the program and what is expected of them to ensure clarity of their goals and responsibilities • If you have a development program that has an "ending point" where participants have completed a group of development components, create a 3-way meeting at the end of the program with you, the participant, and their manager to discuss what the participant learned and applied on the job from the development program • Distribute e-news items, a newsletter, or a web site update to participants on regular basis – this helps keep the program "in front of them" along with their other business priorities. Include reminders, due dates, and upcoming development event dates.
BUSINESS LEADERS	• Incorporate Talent Review and Succession Planning actions with other business actions and events they already have in place; for example, schedule their Talent Review meeting to be part of their quarterly on-site executive staff meeting. • Report business group metrics from your Talent Review process up into overall organizational metrics • Meet with the business leaders at least on semi-annual basis (preferably on a quarterly basis) to discuss progress of action items that they identified during the Talent Review meeting • Set up reward and recognition processes that are tied to the development of people and of succession plans • Ask your CEO or other executive to communicate the importance of developing leadership benchstrength, and to communicate the required participation of all leaders in your Talent Review and Succession Planning process • Meet with leaders on a 1-on-1 basis to review the action plans and progress identified for the business group

Group Name	Accountability Ideas
ORGANIZATION	<ul><li>Include a measured objective within your company's performance review form that pertains to the development of people, including succession planning</li><li>Form a Talent Management committee to serve as sponsors of Executive High Potentials, helping to shape and drive the very high level development actions these individuals will need, such as cross-functional job rotation assignments</li><li>Provide regular e-news, web site information, newsletter articles, etc. in your corporate communications to keep the leadership development programs and options visible in the organization; recognize graduates or participants who applied learning on the job in a significant way</li><li>Provide executive level workshops or "overviews" of the leadership development model and skills that are included in your leadership development programs, so your top level leaders can "speak the language", drive, and support these models and the leadership culture and competencies that the organization values</li><li>Hold large Leadership Development meetings (i.e. by regional location, by business function, by customer or product group) to review progress – this creates a situation in which peers are viewing the ideas and actions implemented by their peers</li></ul>

We've provided several ideas here so you could choose ideas that match your organization's culture, size, and needs. Please don't try to be a hero and do everything at once – choose the accountability ideas that you think will be most important for your company.

Aligning Metrics to Original Goals

When you review the Metrics Checklist later in this section, it is a good idea to also have a summary of your Goals that you identified early on in this book. In most cases, it is necessary to have at least one metric that aligns with your goals – especially for the most critical goals you are trying to accomplish.

As with the Accountability Ideas, remember that it would be better to have a few very important metrics that you are able to follow through with, than a host of metrics that you simply don't have time, resources, or data to complete.

171

When aligning goals with metrics, there are many different ways you can measure the result, which again enables you to choose the one or two methods that will work best in your organization.

For example, if you selected the goal of, "Identify individuals who are fully qualified to fill the incumbent leader's position if it becomes available", then what metrics could apply to measure this? Some ideas include:

- Percentage of leaders with at least one fully qualified successor

- Percentage of leaders with a "3-deep" succession pool of individuals (they have a pool of at least 3 people who are fully ready to step into the position, or they demonstrate the potential to be ready within 1-3 years)

- Measure the "Time-to-Fill" for open leadership positions, comparing 1) the organization's overall time-to-fill metric, 2) positions that had no succession plan, 3) positions that had between one and three potential successors, and 4) positions that had three or more potential successors when the position became vacant

- Measure the frequency in which an individual on the succession plan actually filled an open leadership position that was identified for him or her

> *Remember – don't try to be a hero and implement every accountability idea and every metric – it is better to select a few very important ones that pertain directly to your strategy that you know you will be able to follow through with.*

When selecting metrics that align with your goals, you will also want to identify metrics that will measure results on a variety of levels, from customer feedback results to on-the-job application results to a business return-on-investment, where these are applicable.

While you will probably measure each major component of your Talent Review and Succession Planning process at the customer satisfaction level, it is very unlikely that you will have the time, energy, and resources to measure every component at the return-on-investment level, so choose wisely as you are reviewing the Metrics Checklist with your internal partners.

Using Time Savers – Systems

Another way to increase follow-through with your metrics process is to use systems to help you track and measure results. Now, if your company is using a simple database or spreadsheet software to track your Talent Review and Succession Planning data, please know that you are in good company. In our experience networking with individuals from other companies who have implemented these processes, the majority of them are using these types of software packages to track their leadership data, and that includes many large and sophisticated organizations. So, we are definitely not saying that you need a specific Succession Management or Talent Management system to effectively track and measure your data. We have also used simple spreadsheets to track Talent Review data for years, so it can be done.

BUT, if you have the budget and resources to purchase a system that is specifically designed for talent and succession management, we urge you to do it. A simple Internet search for "succession systems" and "talent systems" will produce a number of vendors who provide these types of tools. While it will certainly take time to implement the system and populate it with your organization's data, it will then pay you back in full through automated reporting functionality and a decrease in reliance on redundant data entry labor.

If you are currently in the market for this type of system, one thing to consider is this question, "Do we define our policies and processes first and then customize a system to match these, or do we purchase a system and define our policies and procedures to match the system?"

And of course the answer depends on your company's readiness, culture, and resources. Our stance is that the best practice is to establish your processes first, to match the needs of your company. But, if this is the first time you are implementing a Talent Review and Succession Planning program, you may benefit greatly from the structure that is already available in the system, and from the advice of the consultants who will help you implement it. Many external talent management systems allow for structured customization and consulting assistance to support your organization's strategy.

Here are some potential questions to consider as you are reviewing automated Succession and/or Talent Management systems:

- The first one that may hit you – what is your budget for the system? This might result in your first elimination of systems provided by some vendors!

- What are the other customers / companies who use this vendor's system? Can you talk with them about their use of and experience with the system?

- Will the system need to have the ability to "talk to" other systems that you have already implemented in your company, such as your Learning Management system, your Human Resources system, your Recruiting / Application Tracking system, etc.

- How user-friendly and intuitive is the system? Especially if your company is medium to large in size, you probably won't be able to provide specific training for your leaders, so purchasing a system that they can work through pretty easily without training may be important to you.

- What reporting capabilities does the system provide? Will the reporting capabilities be able to calculate data you need for the goals and metrics you have chosen for your program?

- What is the typical implementation time that previous customers experienced? What customization is available as part of the initial purchase cost? How are system upgrades priced, if applicable?

- What system implementation and project planning service is provided? What training and documentation is provided with the system?

Using Time Savers – People Ideas

Whether or not you have a specialized Succession or Talent Management system, there are other ways you can make the metrics process a little easier. One method is to place more of the responsibility for measurement on the development participants; after all, they are the ones who are benefiting from the development and are responsible for learning and on-the-job application.

For example, require each participant of a leadership development program to identify at least one business metric they will be responsible for reporting on at the end of the program that will be enhanced through the learning process (this is typically not applicable for participants of a single workshop).

Especially for participants who show promising initial results, but are having trouble turning it into an ROI metric, you may need to meet with them to help them work through this process.

For example, you have two leadership program participants who did not know each other prior to participating in the program. During the program, they built a relationship and learned some new process ideas, and began discussing a change in procedure between their two departments that would increase efficiency, and ultimately they implement the new process.

You then meet with these two individuals to help identify where the cost savings or additional revenue was achieved – can the speed of the new process be measured against the previous process time, with this time savings then multiplied by the average hourly salary of each employee in both departments? Multiply this calculation by the increase in work hour production for all employees for an entire year, and you have the annual cost savings. Subtract your training expenses, and you have your annual ROI calculation.

Another possibility is that your internal HR and business partners may already have metrics that they are responsible for that you can also use to measure results, without any new calculations on your part, or with minimal calculating and analyzing.

For example, if your Recruiting department already calculates the average "time-to-fill" for leadership positions, you have a metric you can use. If your legal department already tracks the number of employee calls to your integrity or sexual harassment hotline, you can break this data up and compare leaders who participated in leadership development programs versus those who did not, and the difference between the number of or the percentage of hotline calls. If your human resources department already measures employee retention, you can compare the retention of leaders who have completed leadership development programs versus those who have not.

Communicating Results

Publicize the results of your Talent Review and Succession Planning process using the methods most appropriate for the information you want to convey:

- Use your company web site, newsletter, and e-news forums to reward and recognize leadership development participants, leaders who excel at employee development, and case study human interest stories of individuals or work groups that have demonstrated enhanced business results from new knowledge, skills, and leadership abilities

- Use executive summaries and executive talent review presentations to convey company-wide results to senior leaders

- Work with business group leaders to obtain an agenda item on their regular staff meetings to report progress and results

- Report business results to your internal partners so they can answer questions about the progress of leadership development in the company, and to equip them to communicate results as they are talking with leaders daily

- With the approval of your company, publish your results and/or best practices in industry periodicals – this provides good "PR" for your company!

- Present your best practices and results at industry conferences to increase visibility of your organization's commitment to leadership excellence

Presenting Results to Your Sponsors

Once again, we'd like to save you some "brain time" and provide some general sample slides in this chapter that may be applicable for you to customize to your company for a presentation of the results of your Talent Review and Succession Planning process.

Of course, a final results presentation will be different for every organization; these generic slides are simply designed to help you get started. You will need to customize, add, and delete slides from this sample set as needed to fully present your organization's leadership development accomplishments and progress.

An easy way to get started on the topics to cover in your presentation is to ensure that you are presenting the results of each of the goals you targeted for the process.

For example, if you decided to identify high potentials in your organization, you will want to include a slide on the resulting numbers, percentages, etc. of the individuals who were selected for your high potential program.

If you decided to identify "vacancy risk" of incumbent leaders in your organization, you will want to include a chart that identifies the percentages of risk within the organization, and if needed, you will want to present data that breaks this high level information down into more detail, such as a high vacancy risk that you identified in a specific geographic location that is part of your overall organization.

Sample Results Presentation Slides

Leadership Population Data

- Overall leadership population
  - Numbers
  - Percentages
  - By leadership category
  - By geographic location (if applicable)
  - Ratio of leaders to employees

Talent Review Actions

- Number of leaders reviewed during the Talent Review process
  - Overall
  - By Business Group
  - By Location
- Categories of leaders reviewed
- Overall results and/or feedback from leaders

Talent Review Results

- (Note: Depending on your results and your audience, each of the following items may need to be a graph on separate slides)

- Leadership Benchstrength Data, i.e.

  – Number / Percentage of Open Leadership Positions

  – Current Time-to-Fill for Leadership Positions

  – Talent Pool Data

- Vacancy Risk Results

- Vacancy Risk compared to Succession Plan Strength

- Job Assignment Results (National and/or Global Placements)

High Potential Population

- Status of notification and/or development

- Results from previous years (i.e. performance measures, retention, promotional rate, etc.)

- Number of high potentials (by category, if applicable)

- Percentage of the population

- Current development plans for the high potential population

Succession Planning Results

- Estimation of Leadership Turnover in the Coming Year

- Percentage of successors available:

    - By Senior Leader / Business Group

    - By Successor Readiness Category

- Any Significant Succession Plan Gaps Identified

- Succession Plan Strengths

Recommendations

- Overall "themes" from the Talent Review discussions

- Gaps / areas of development identified, and recommended actions

- Areas of leadership benchstrength gains and strengths to celebrate

- Sponsor / Executive Support Needed

- What's Next

The Next Step

While we all probably wish our organization would just clap their hands and say, "I believe in training and organizational development" in a Peter Pan fashion, the fact is we need to continue to prove and improve our development products and services as any business group must do.

The next step is to create your metrics plan, using the Metrics Checklist on the following pages. This tool will help you to identify the metrics you can implement immediately, the metrics you need to obtain, organize, and analyze, the metrics you might implement in the future as your program becomes more established, and the metrics that do not apply to your organization. From this process you can then create a summary plan of the items you will be measuring and the data you need to obtain.

Metrics Checklist

The metrics you will calculate during and after the Talent Review process will provide information to your business leaders about the overall status and strength of their leadership teams, as well as the entire organization. The data gathered over time will also indicate whether the program is providing a return-on-investment to the organization, the areas of shortening the "time-to-fill" for open leadership positions, reducing the transition or learning period for new leaders, reducing turnover of the leadership population, etc.

At the beginning of this book, you identified the unique goals of your Talent Assessment and Succession Planning process, to match your organization's needs, using a checklist approach. Similarly, use this Metrics Checklist to identify the unique measurement needs of your organization.

Use the following rating scale to identify the metrics you already have available in your company, the metrics you want to add now to your Talent Review and Succession Planning Process, metrics that you may want to add in the future, and the metrics that are not applicable to your organization.

Rating Scale and Definitions:

1 = Metrics already measured and available in your organization

2 = Metrics to add now to our Talent Review and Succession Planning process

3 = Metrics you may want to add in the future to your process

4 = Metrics that are not applicable to your organization

This Metrics Checklist includes a large number and wide variety of potential metrics that can be used to measure talent management and leadership development.

Choose a manageable number of metrics that you will be able to realistically implement. Identify the metrics that align with your organizational needs and expectations.

A Three-Step Metrics Planning Process

This Metrics Checklist tool provides a three-step process to define, plan, and follow through with the measurement of your Talent Review and Succession Planning program:

Step One: Use the rating system shown on the previous page to identify the applicability of each of the metric choices listed on the following pages.

Step Two: Summarize the metrics you are currently using (or you have the data available and you simply need to analyze it) and the metrics you want to add to your measurement process, using the summary tables in this chapter. This will provide a concise list of the metrics you have chosen, how you will obtain each metric, and how often you will review or analyze each one.

Step Three: The most challenging aspect of metrics is typically the ongoing follow-through that is required to demonstrate results. Program evaluation is critical but often doesn't make the top of the "urgent things to do" list. The last part of this chapter provides ideas you can use to help increase accountability in your evaluation process.

General Leadership Population Metrics

These metrics are general measurements we recommend to provide an overview of your organization's leadership population, to watch for trends such as changes in leadership job titles/positions, ratio of leaders per employee, etc. Significant changes in these trends should be reviewed to ensure the overall leadership population continues to meet the needs of the changing organization.

Ratings:

1 = Metrics already measured and available in your organization

2 = Metrics to add now to our Talent Review and Succession Planning process

3 = Metrics you may want to add in the future to your process

4 = Metrics that are not applicable to your organization

1	2	3	4	
☐	☐	☐	☐	Number of individuals in the organization who are in a leadership position (with staff reporting to them)
☐	☐	☐	☐	Number of and percentage of leaders categorized by title (i.e. supervisor, manager, director, etc.)
☐	☐	☐	☐	Changes in the percentage of leaders by job title, from one year to the next, (to identify any trends in leadership population growth)
☐	☐	☐	☐	Average performance ratings:

- Leadership population compared to overall population
- Leadership population broken out by job title
- Overall organization
- By business group
- High potentials compared to overall population
- Comparing performance ratings of high potential population from year to year, during development program
- By location or country

☐	☐	☐	☐	Diversity / gender statistics of leadership population (overall population and by job title category)

General Leadership Population Metrics (Continued)

Ratings:

1 = Metrics already measured and available in your organization

2 = Metrics to add now to our Talent Review and Succession Planning process

3 = Metrics you may want to add in the future to your process

4 = Metrics that are not applicable to your organization

1	2	3	4	
❑	❑	❑	❑	Percentage of leadership population compared to overall organizational population:

- Total company percentage of leaders compared to the "all employee population"

- Percentage by business unit (expect a higher leadership population percentage in business groups with a larger number of exempt employees)

1	2	3	4	
❑	❑	❑	❑	Average number of employees per leader
❑	❑	❑	❑	Average length of tenure per leader
❑	❑	❑	❑	Percentage of leaders who have been in their position less than 6 months / less than 1 year
❑	❑	❑	❑	Leadership population data by country, region, city, etc.

Leadership Development Metrics

These metrics provide data regarding the overall effectiveness of your leadership development programs, resources, and actions. These metrics are an important part of your measurement of the Talent Review and Succession Planning process, because they pertain to the use of leadership development resources you are providing within your organization to help leaders leverage their strengths and grow in their development areas, as defined during your talent review process. These metrics "tell the story" of how effective the overall leadership development process is in your organization.

Ratings:

1 = Metrics already measured and available in your organization

2 = Metrics to add now to our Talent Review and Succession Planning process

3 = Metrics you may want to add in the future to your process

4 = Metrics that are not applicable to your organization

1	2	3	4	
☐	☐	☐	☐	Number of / percentage of leaders who have a written development plan in place
☐	☐	☐	☐	Number of / percentage of leaders who have discussed their career and development plan with their own leader
☐	☐	☐	☐	Percentage of completion of development plan action items annually
☐	☐	☐	☐	Satisfaction ratings and comments from participants of leadership development workshops, e-learning courses, and users of other leadership development resources available in the organization
☐	☐	☐	☐	Satisfaction ratings and comments from leaders regarding their knowledge of what leadership resources are available to them and how to obtain the resources
☐	☐	☐	☐	Completion rates of participants in workshops, e-learning courses, and other leadership development resources available
☐	☐	☐	☐	Cancellation rates of registrants in workshops, e-learning courses, and other leadership development resources available

Leadership Development Metrics (Continued)

Ratings:

> **1 = Metrics already measured and available in your organization**
>
> **2 = Metrics to add now to our Talent Review and Succession Planning process**
>
> **3 = Metrics you may want to add in the future to your process**
>
> **4 = Metrics that are not applicable to your organization**

1	2	3	4	
❏	❏	❏	❏	Assessment scores of leadership knowledge and skills (i.e. on-the-job skill assessments, workshop testing, practice, or assessments, etc.)
❏	❏	❏	❏	Length of transition period for newly hired and newly promoted leaders
❏	❏	❏	❏	Demonstrated behavioral improvements in strength leverage and development areas of individuals who have completed development actions (as measured through before and after assessments, case studies, interviews, etc.)
❏	❏	❏	❏	Return-on-investment studies pertaining to specific leadership development programs, business groups, projects, etc.

Leadership Benchstrength and Succession Plan Metrics

These metrics provide indicators regarding the strength of your leadership pipeline, your potential leadership turnover predictions, and the strength of the succession plans for leadership positions.

Ratings:

    1 = Metrics already measured and available in your organization

    2 = Metrics to add now to our Talent Review and Succession Planning process

    3 = Metrics you may want to add in the future to your process

    4 = Metrics that are not applicable to your organization

1	2	3	4	
❑	❑	❑	❑	Number of / percentage of leaders approaching an "eligibility of retirement age" in the organization
❑	❑	❑	❑	Comparison of leadership population at "high risk" of leaving the organization, compared to the strength of the prepared successor pool, to identify areas with expected higher turnover but with weaker succession pools
❑	❑	❑	❑	Percentage of time succession plan candidate fills incumbent position
❑	❑	❑	❑	Identification of "multi-successors", who are successors to multiple positions in the organization
❑	❑	❑	❑	Number of / percentage of successors who are in a different location from the incumbent they would be succeeding
❑	❑	❑	❑	Number of / percentage of successors who are in a different business unit from the incumbent they would be succeeding (measures the level to which the organization is successful at identifying "cross-functional" successors
❑	❑	❑	❑	Risk of Leaving percentages – high risk, moderate risk, low risk
❑	❑	❑	❑	Impact to the Organization (if the individual does leave the organization)

187

Leadership Benchstrength and Succession Plan Metrics (Continued)

Ratings:

    1 = Metrics already measured and available in your organization

    2 = Metrics to add now to our Talent Review and Succession Planning process

    3 = Metrics you may want to add in the future to your process

    4 = Metrics that are not applicable to your organization

1	2	3	4	
☐	☐	☐	☐	Identification of leaders who are ready for a lateral or promotional career move
☐	☐	☐	☐	Estimation of leadership turnover expected in the coming year based on retirement eligibility figures, high risk of leaving figures, performance improvement figures, etc.
☐	☐	☐	☐	Internal candidate versus external candidate fill of leadership positions; measure the: - Organizational-wide candidate fill percentages - Percentages by business group - Percentages by location - Percentages within each leadership title category (i.e. supervisor, manager, director, etc.)
☐	☐	☐	☐	Number of candidates who are defined as ready to fill positions that have been identified as critical to the organization
☐	☐	☐	☐	Percentage of successors available: - by leader - by business unit - by category of successor

High Potential Population Metrics

These metrics are important to gather to ensure your high potential population meets your organization's guidelines and needs, and to track trends and changes in your high potential population from year to year.

Ratings:

  1 = Metrics already measured and available in your organization

  2 = Metrics to add now to our Talent Review and Succession Planning process

  3 = Metrics you may want to add in the future to your process

  4 = Metrics that are not applicable to your organization

1	2	3	4	
❏	❏	❏	❏	Number of high potentials and percentage of high potential population compared to the candidate pool population
❏	❏	❏	❏	Percentage of high potential population: - by business group - by location or country
❏	❏	❏	❏	Number of main experts and percentage of individuals in the critical expert population compared to the candidate pool population
❏	❏	❏	❏	Number of individuals in each high potential category (if applicable)
❏	❏	❏	❏	Percentage of individuals in each high potential category compared to overall high potential population
❏	❏	❏	❏	Number of / percentage of high potentials based on number of years in the program (i.e. first year participants, second year participants, etc.)
❏	❏	❏	❏	Percentage of high potentials who are also successors (this percentage should be high to help ensure high potentials have at least one potential future career option

High Potential Population Metrics (Continued)

These metrics are important to gather to ensure your high potential population meets your organization's guidelines and needs, and to track trends and changes in your high potential population from year to year.

Ratings:

1 = Metrics already measured and available in your organization

2 = Metrics to add now to our Talent Review and Succession Planning process

3 = Metrics you may want to add in the future to your process

4 = Metrics that are not applicable to your organization

1	2	3	4	
☐	☐	☐	☐	Number of / percentage of individuals who declined participation in the high potential program
☐	☐	☐	☐	Number of / percentage of individuals who have been removed from the high potential program from the previous year
☐	☐	☐	☐	Diversity / gender statistics of high potential population
☐	☐	☐	☐	Percentage of successors who are also high potentials
☐	☐	☐	☐	Number of / percentage of high potentials who completed development action requirements each year

Talent Review Meeting Metrics

These metrics are designed to define and measure the activity involved in the Talent Review process for the current year. These metrics can be helpful in determining staffing needs for the Talent Review process, as well as predicting the amount of time that will need to be devoted each year to the Talent Review process. These metrics also provide indicators regarding the effectiveness of your Talent Review process, and can provide data that will help you improve your process from year to year.

Ratings:

1 = Metrics already measured and available in your organization

2 = Metrics to add now to our Talent Review and Succession Planning process

3 = Metrics you may want to add in the future to your process

4 = Metrics that are not applicable to your organization

1	2	3	4	
☐	☐	☐	☐	Number of employees reviewed during the Talent Assessment process
☐	☐	☐	☐	Number of leaders reviewed during Talent Review meetings
☐	☐	☐	☐	Level one evaluation feedback from leaders who participated in the Talent Review meetings
☐	☐	☐	☐	Average length of Talent Review meeting, compared to number of leaders reviewed
☐	☐	☐	☐	Level one (initial customer satisfaction) evaluation feedback from leaders who participated in the Talent Assessment process
☐	☐	☐	☐	Evaluation feedback from internal partners on the entire Talent Review and Succession Planning process – HR, etc.
☐	☐	☐	☐	Number of / percentage of business groups that completed a Talent Review process in the past year

Talent Review Return-on-Investment Metrics

These metrics have the potential to demonstrate the business and financial return-on-investment from your Talent Review and Succession Planning process.

Ratings:

1 = Metrics already measured and available in your organization

2 = Metrics to add now to our Talent Review and Succession Planning process

3 = Metrics you may want to add in the future to your process

4 = Metrics that are not applicable to your organization

1	2	3	4	
☐	☐	☐	☐	Time to Fill – Leadership Positions (measure differences at multiple levels)
☐	☐	☐	☐	Internal vs. External leadership position fill (use to measure cost savings due to reduced external recruiter fees, external position advertisement costs, etc.)
☐	☐	☐	☐	Performance Improvement percentage within leadership population
☐	☐	☐	☐	Length of transition time period for newly promoted leaders
☐	☐	☐	☐	Turnover of leadership population
☐	☐	☐	☐	Turnover of successors
☐	☐	☐	☐	Turnover of high potential population
☐	☐	☐	☐	Recruiting cost per leadership hire (break out data by levels, i.e. supervisors, managers, directors, vice presidents, executives)
☐	☐	☐	☐	Number of / percentage of high potentials who took a lateral career move in the last year
☐	☐	☐	☐	Number of / percentage of high potentials who took a promotional career move in the last year

Talent Review Return-on-Investment Metrics (Continued)

Ratings:

    1 = Metrics already measured and available in your organization

    2 = Metrics to add now to our Talent Review and Succession Planning process

    3 = Metrics you may want to add in the future to your process

    4 = Metrics that are not applicable to your organization

1   2   3   4

☐   ☐   ☐   ☐   Comparison of the job performance of high potential leaders to general population based on your business metrics, such as:

- Financial Metrics, such as Revenue / Profit & Loss data / Budget Compliance / Expense Control

- Customer data – i.e. satisfaction ratings, customer retention, numbers of new customers, etc.

- Employee Engagement survey results

- Employee Turnover

- Employee Development measurements – i.e. career moves, competency database skill building, etc.

☐   ☐   ☐   ☐   Percentage of high potentials who say that notification and participation in the high potential development program influenced their decision to stay with / grow with the company

☐   ☐   ☐   ☐   Evaluation feedback and on-the-job results from high potential individuals regarding their development program

☐   ☐   ☐   ☐   Number of / percentage of high potentials who have a written development plan in place

☐   ☐   ☐   ☐   Number of / percentage of successors who have a written development plan in place

☐   ☐   ☐   ☐   Number of / percentage of Talent Review action plans completed each year

Location or Global Leadership Metrics

These metrics will provide data that will be helpful when determining leadership needs or gaps based on geographic needs, which are especially important for organizations with significant geographic spread over the national and/or global market.

Ratings:

    1 = Metrics already measured and available in your organization

    2 = Metrics to add now to our Talent Review and Succession Planning process

    3 = Metrics you may want to add in the future to your process

    4 = Metrics that are not applicable to your organization

1	2	3	4	
☐	☐	☐	☐	Number of / percentage of leaders (and/or high potentials) who are currently working in an expatriate job assignment each year
☐	☐	☐	☐	Number of / percentage of leaders who have relocated within the country each year
☐	☐	☐	☐	Number of / percentage of leaders who are waiting for / ready for a new national or international job assignment
☐	☐	☐	☐	Percentage of leaders within different cities, regions, and/or countries populated by the organization
☐	☐	☐	☐	Number of and percentage of high potential employees by city, region, or country

Summary of Metrics Decisions

Use this space to summarize the metrics you rated on the previous pages of this chapter. Summarize the metrics you already have in place that you can use to measure your programs, as well as the new metrics you need to gather and use for your Talent Review and Succession Planning evaluation processes.

Summary of Items Rated as "1" Metrics already measured and available in your organization		
Metric Description	**Source of Metric Data**	**Metric Analysis Frequency**
		❑ Quarterly ❑ Bi-Annually ❑ Annually ❑ Other _____
		❑ Quarterly ❑ Bi-Annually ❑ Annually ❑ Other _____
		❑ Quarterly ❑ Bi-Annually ❑ Annually ❑ Other _____
		❑ Quarterly ❑ Bi-Annually ❑ Annually ❑ Other _____
		❑ Quarterly ❑ Bi-Annually ❑ Annually ❑ Other _____

Summary of Items Rated as "1"		
Metrics already measured and available in your organization		
Metric Description	**Source of Metric Data**	**Metric Analysis Frequency**
		❑ Quarterly ❑ Bi-Annually ❑ Annually ❑ Other _____
		❑ Quarterly ❑ Bi-Annually ❑ Annually ❑ Other _____
		❑ Quarterly ❑ Bi-Annually ❑ Annually ❑ Other _____
		❑ Quarterly ❑ Bi-Annually ❑ Annually ❑ Other _____
		❑ Quarterly ❑ Bi-Annually ❑ Annually ❑ Other _____
		❑ Quarterly ❑ Bi-Annually ❑ Annually ❑ Other _____

Summary of Items Rated as "1"		
Metrics already measured and available in your organization		
Metric Description	**Source of Metric Data**	**Metric Analysis Frequency**
		❑ Quarterly ❑ Bi-Annually ❑ Annually ❑ Other _____
		❑ Quarterly ❑ Bi-Annually ❑ Annually ❑ Other _____
		❑ Quarterly ❑ Bi-Annually ❑ Annually ❑ Other _____
		❑ Quarterly ❑ Bi-Annually ❑ Annually ❑ Other _____
		❑ Quarterly ❑ Bi-Annually ❑ Annually ❑ Other _____
		❑ Quarterly ❑ Bi-Annually ❑ Annually ❑ Other _____

Summary of Items Rated as "2" **Metrics to Add Now to Our Talent Review and Succession Planning process**		
Metric Description	**Source of Metric Data**	**Metric Analysis Frequency**
		❑ Quarterly ❑ Bi-Annually ❑ Annually ❑ Other _____
		❑ Quarterly ❑ Bi-Annually ❑ Annually ❑ Other _____
		❑ Quarterly ❑ Bi-Annually ❑ Annually ❑ Other _____
		❑ Quarterly ❑ Bi-Annually ❑ Annually ❑ Other _____
		❑ Quarterly ❑ Bi-Annually ❑ Annually ❑ Other _____
		❑ Quarterly ❑ Bi-Annually ❑ Annually ❑ Other _____

Summary of Items Rated as "2" Metrics to Add Now to Our Talent Review and Succession Planning process		
Metric Description	**Source of Metric Data**	**Metric Analysis Frequency**
		❑ Quarterly ❑ Bi-Annually ❑ Annually ❑ Other _____
		❑ Quarterly ❑ Bi-Annually ❑ Annually ❑ Other _____
		❑ Quarterly ❑ Bi-Annually ❑ Annually ❑ Other _____
		❑ Quarterly ❑ Bi-Annually ❑ Annually ❑ Other _____
		❑ Quarterly ❑ Bi-Annually ❑ Annually ❑ Other _____
		❑ Quarterly ❑ Bi-Annually ❑ Annually ❑ Other _____

Summary of Items Rated as "2" Metrics to Add Now to Our Talent Review and Succession Planning process		
Metric Description	**Source of Metric Data**	**Metric Analysis Frequency**
		❏ Quarterly ❏ Bi-Annually ❏ Annually ❏ Other _____
		❏ Quarterly ❏ Bi-Annually ❏ Annually ❏ Other _____
		❏ Quarterly ❏ Bi-Annually ❏ Annually ❏ Other _____
		❏ Quarterly ❏ Bi-Annually ❏ Annually ❏ Other _____
		❏ Quarterly ❏ Bi-Annually ❏ Annually ❏ Other _____
		❏ Quarterly ❏ Bi-Annually ❏ Annually ❏ Other _____

Making It Happen

Congratulations! You've completed your metrics planning. We know that unless you have a particular affinity for and interest in measurement (i.e. you are a tailor, a scientist, or an inchworm), this section may have been somewhat tedious and challenging for you, so give yourself a pat on the back.

So we know you are ready to leave all of this and go out and have some fun! Before you do that, take a few more minutes to think about what you are going to do to follow through on your metrics plans to obtain, analyze, and report on the data. Here are some ideas you could use to help with your follow-through strategy:

☐ Form a cross-functional metrics committee that meets on a specific frequency basis (i.e. monthly, quarterly, etc.) to review measurement progress and results

☐ Set up an accountability process in which you are required to report metrics results at least annually on a formal basis to your leadership or executive team

☐ Create a metrics web site to record and share metrics data

☐ Join one of the many human resources or training industry benchmarking forums to submit your metrics data and obtain comparison data and reports

☐ Include a metrics performance review objective for each employee who contributes to the measurement process

☐ Purchase a tool or system that is designed to automate, store, and report on your metrics data

☐ Set up an organizational scorecard of business metrics that include a one or two of your most critical metrics regarding leadership benchstrength

Project Summary Tool

Use this tool to create a summary of all of the decisions you made as you worked through this book to put together your Talent Management and Succession planning project. Review your "Checkpoint" responses in the Planning Section of this book, and compile your results here. Once you complete this tool, you can use it for your own tracking purposes, and you can use it as a part of your communication package.

Project Sponsors (Name and Title)

Project Team

Team Member	Role / Responsibilities

Overall Purpose or Vision for our Talent Management Strategy

First Year Goals

Metrics to Measure Goal Progress and Success

Definitions

Term / Topic	Our Organization's Definition / Parameters
High Potential	
Successor	
Critical Expert	
Talent Assessment	
Talent Review Meeting	

Readiness Checklist Summary: Strengths and Potential Challenges

Key Strengths	Critical Challenges to Address

Potential Obstacles – Contingency Plans

What potential obstacles do we anticipate that could impede implementation of Talent Management into our organization's culture successfully?

Potential Obstacle	Contingency Plan to Reduce / Eliminate Obstacle

Motivational Forces – Leveraging Our Strengths

What positive forces and strengths will help us drive the implementation of Talent Management into our organization's culture successfully?	
Positive Force	How We Can Leverage This Force

Vendors and External Resources

Vendor / Resource Name and Contact Information	Role / Purpose

Internal Partners

Name / Department	Role / Purpose

Our Notification Decisions

Notification Question	Decision / Notes
Will we notify high potentials that they have been selected for the program?	
Will we provide a formal development program for high potentials, or will the managers of high potentials be responsible for their development?	
Will we notify successors that they have been identified as such?	
Will we provide a formal development program for successors, or will the managers of successors be responsible for their development?	
Will we notify other employees of the results of the talent assessment process?	

Our System / Data Storage Decisions

System / Data Storage Question	Decision / Notes
Will we use a paper-based, PC software based, or web-based tool for talent assessment?	
Will we use a paper-based, PC software based, or web-based tool for the storage and ongoing use of talent management and succession planning data?	

Accountability Methods

What internal processes, recognition, and rewards will we implement to build Talent Management into our culture and hold leaders accountable for people development?

Communication Tools

What communication tools do we currently have in place (or that we can implement) to communicate the Talent Management and Succession Planning process in the company?	
Communication Tool	Notes / Use of Tool

First Year Timeline

	Identify the milestones planned for the first year of implementation:	
Month	Milestone Description / Notes	Lead Project Team Member
January		
February		
March		
April		
May		
June		
July		
August		
September		
October		
November		
December		
2nd Year Milestones:		

Congratulations! Your decision-making process and project plan are now complete, and you are ready to execute your program. Remember this is a marathon and not a sprint – keep moving forward steadily with your plans. Good luck!

Index

Printed in the United States
87921LV00003B/129-220/A